The Competitive Edge III

With harmony between horse and rider, dressage becomes an art. *The late Col. Hans Handler, Director, The Spanish Riding School, Vienna.*

THE COMPETITIVE EDGE III

GRAVITY, BALANCE AND KINETICS OF THE HORSE AND RIDER

BY MAX GAHWYLER

HALF HALT PRESS, INC.
BOONSBORO, MARYLAND

The Competitive Edge III:
Gravity, Balance and Kinetics of the Horse and Rider
©2000 Dr. Max Gahwyler

Published in
the United States of America by
Half Halt Press, Inc.
P. O. Box 67
Boonsboro, MD 21713
www.halfhaltpress.com

All rights reserved. No part of this book may be reproduced in
any way or by any means without permission
in writing from the publisher.

Printed in the United States of America

Cartoons and illustrations by
Patricia Peyman Naegeli
Editorial services by Samantha Harrison
Photos on page 109 from **Bits, Bridles and Saddles** by Doris
Culshaw. Used by permission of Chrysalis Book Group.

Library of Congress Cataloging-in-Publication Data

Gahwyler, Max, 1923-
　The competitive edge III : gravity, balance, and kinetics of the horse and rider / by Max Gahwyler.
　　p. cm.
　ISBN 0-939481-59-6 (hardcover)
　1. Horsemanship. I. Title: Competitive edge 3. II. Title: Competitive edge three. III. Title.
SF309 .G19 2000
798.2--dc21
　　　　　　　　　　　　　　　　　　　　　　　　　　00-047202

TABLE OF CONTENTS

Introduction		1
Chapter 1	Gravity and Balance	7
Chapter 2	Timing	33
Chapter 3	Center of Mass	41
Chapter 4	The Origin of Biokinetics and the Central Nervous System	53
Chapter 5	Human Kinetics: Based on Gravity and Center of Mass in Relation to Balance	61
Chapter 6	Human Biomechanics and the Seat	77
Chapter 7	The Lower Spine	91
Chapter 8	The Seat and the Saddle	101
Chapter 9	The Three Gaits of Human and Horse	111
Chapter 10	The Effect of Weight, the Most Sophisticated Aid	139
Epilogue		153

INTRODUCTION

Riding is a dual challenge for most of us. It is first of all a physical challenge to accomplish integration and coordination and harmony with the horse. And it is an intellectual challenge to try to understand what we are doing. These two challenges have existed for a very, very long time as demonstrated by innumerable books written through the ages.

Even with the large numbers of new "how-to" books which come out every year, along with the many magazines such as *Dressage Today*, *Practical Horseman*, and so many others, plus all the clinics, symposiums and speeches, we are still struggling with what we are doing!

In this book I will not try to answer the question, "What to do?" or instruct you how to pull here, push there, sit a little deeper, etc. Rather, the purpose of this book is to explore why we still have all these troubles in our riding, and why we haven't solved the problems after 10,000 years of human beings riding. I hope that if we understand the issues behind the problems, we can better solve them.

Take the following example, that of a teenager learning to drive a car. Within a few hours of learning and practice, he is perfectly at ease and has no problem driving around. But put that same teenager on a horse and you have a totally disorganized individual who cannot control his balance, his hands or his legs. You are just happy if he doesn't fall off the horse! You wouldn't even consider letting him canter or anything else that involved his balance.

Similarly, around 10,000 years ago we started as a species to ride and now, 10,000 years later, we still cannot automatically do it. The reason for the difficulty is kinetics.

Kinetics refers to the branch of science that considers the movements of an entity (such as human or a horse). For our purposes, we're considering kinetics to be the study of human and equine motion and movement, which are both based on the necessity of coping with the forces of gravity.

The kinetics of horse and human are vastly different. Man changed his way of moving when he started to move about upright, using his brain to make weapons and tools. He no longer relied on gaits for speed either for pursuit or for escape, since he had only one gait—one foot after the other. As a matter of fact, most of us can't even run as fast as a Jack Russell Terrier. But the horse continues to work on four legs with a great variation of different gaits and combinations thereof.

Going back to the example of a car, the entire machinery is built exclusively to accommodate human kinetics. It is a very fine science, the designing of the car to fit the human. When you sit in a car, you automatically feel completely at ease.

However, in riding it is just the opposite. The kinetics of horse and human simply do not match and, in most instances, are contradictory to each other. So in order to ride, we either try to force our kinetics on the horse, which never works, or we make a huge effort to gradually acquire the reflexes and coordination that suit the horse.

What is the reason for these different kinetics between horse and human? The answer is gravity. Our kinetics of moving, like everything else on this earth, is determined by gravity. Or, to put it another way, kinetics is a body's response to gravity. Living with gravity is the environment in which we exist, even if we hardly ever give it a thought.

Just a few examples: if you want to pour yourself a cup of coffee to drink, you can only do it because of gravity. If you drive a car downhill, you need to apply brakes. If you go uphill, you have to step on the gas. Even just simply sitting on a chair is only possible because of gravity.

The rain falls down and rivers flow downhill. When skiing, you can go easily downhill using gravity. Uphill, you must climb by yourself or you must take the lift. In the rising trot, the fact that you come back to the saddle is because of gravity.

If you fall on the stairs, you finish at the bottom, not at the top. While riding, if you drop a glove you must get off the horse to get it because it's not going to float back up to you. When you jump a fence, hopefully you land on the other side because of gravity. Even when you put down the phone, it is the weight of the receiver that interrupts the telephone conversation.

So, once you really look at it, there is absolutely nothing that escapes gravity, and everything on this earth has to adjust to these forces.

Therefore, the kinetics of any individual has the simple objective to maintain the body in balance. If you don't, you fall down! The kinetics we acquire while growing up, from our time as a little child to being a toddler, and then beginning to go about steadily on our feet, are simply to manage this gravity. We all do it a little differently as we go along.

What also happens is that once we acquire these reflexes, we are completely unaware of them. Just stand up and then try to analyze the roughly one 100 muscles you used to do it. You will quickly realize that you have no idea how you accomplished it.

This basic fact has been described by Moshe Feldenkreis, the most famous kinesiologist of the early 20th century. His work is one of the main influences on such well known personalities as Linda Tellington-Jones. (As an aside, his book **Awareness Through Movement** is worth reading for more on this topic.)

So, we are not aware of our own movements to maintain this balance. However, it's quite clear that while we get on a horse without knowing how we move ourselves, we still try to tell the horse how to move. This is where many of the problems of riding come in.

And since the human species is not going to change very much and horses are not going to change very much, even 10,000 years from now humans will probably not be better riders than they are today or were 10,000 years ago, despite being enormously richer in advice and suggestions that have been formulated through the years.

Everyone who starts out learning to ride must start at the beginning. There are no short cuts.

So let's look at horses and humans and how they stay on their feet and their ways of coping with this fundamental fact of gravity. To put it simply, let's compare their kinetics.

This is not such an outlandish thought. As in other sports, the study of human kinetics has allowed tremendous progress in the last 30 years and has become an integral part of instruction in golf, swimming, tennis, ice skating, gymnastics and skiing. The studies have even gone so far as to distinguish between the kinetics of men, woman and children and their physical options and potential. Most professional sports instructors are now aware of these issues.

In examining the effects of gravity in the following chapters, my goal is to give you another approach that I hope will make you think and try to assess what's happening in your riding. Understanding why we cannot instantly become accomplished riders allows us to focus on those areas which are the root of the problem.

It will also help us decide what to do about it and explain why it takes such time and patience to learn to ride.

In this book, we will look at riding from this perspective only and relate everything to gravity, the center of mass and kinetics.

I fully realize that this book is not an in-depth study of the subject and is very "one-topic" oriented; it doesn't hold all the answers to your riding problems. More knowledgeable people may even take exception to some of the statements. But if it creates some impetus and more discussion on this long-neglected subject, it will have more than accomplished its purpose.

Gravity is a pain in the ___!

CHAPTER 1

GRAVITY AND BALANCE

There is probably no book on the subject of riding and hardly a magazine article that does not refer to balance, admonishing us to keep the horse balanced, to be in balance with the horse, to stay balanced in the movements, or to use our balance to influence the horse, etc., etc.

But when you ask, "What *is* balance?" you'll rarely get an answer that makes sense. Nor will you often find a useful explanation in the literature on exactly what balance is and how the horse copes with it, or what the effect of the rider is on this phenomenon.

The *Webster's Dictionary* definition says: *Balance is to keep equilibrium on a narrow base*, and the definition of equilibrium is *equality of weight or force....A state where an organism is normally oriented to its environment.*

This is very interesting but it really does not explain anything, especially if we wish to apply it to a moving, four-legged animal carrying a package on its back, over which it has no control, except to maybe buck it off.

Let's look at the basic facts of balance, and consider the individual components that are important:

1. The gravitational pull the earth exerts on any object on its surface: nothing and nobody can escape it.

2. The forces opposing the gravitational pull must be equal to the force of gravity to keep any object in a steady position.

3. The center of gravity is the point in any mass which, if supported by a single upward force equal to the pull of gravity, will keep the total mass in a status quo or equilibrium.

4. In order for an object to remain upright, a vertical line from the center of gravity must fall within the area of support. If this line falls outside the base, the object will topple over.

Therefore, an object can be called "in balance" when its center of gravity remains within its base of support, and the supporting forces are equal to the gravitational pull. (This obviously does not apply to your checkbook where other parameters prevail!)

VARIATIONS OF BALANCE

There is room for significant variations within this definition that have a fundamental importance in riding. Let's examine the following simplistic examples to make the point.

Take a pyramid and put it on a flat surface and you have three options of balance.

A
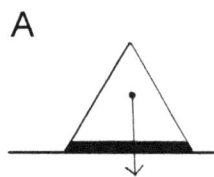

The center of gravity supported by a broad base. The broader the base, the more difficult to push the object off its base.

The lower the center of gravity and the broader the base of support, the more the balance is stable.

This is stable balance.

A body can stay like this indefinitely.

B
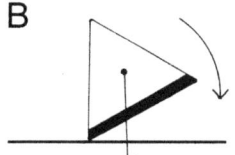

The base has shifted to one point. The center of gravity is still within the original base of support.

If no other interference occurs, the pyramid will fall back to position A.

This is unstable balance.

It will correct itself if allowed to do so, returning to its original stable balance.

C
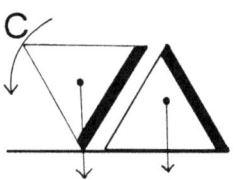

The center of gravity is outside base of support. The pyramid will topple, finishing in a new state of stable balance but upside down.

This is off balance.

Off balance always leads to a new stable balance.

Taking this example a step further, let's repeat the same experiment but put the pyramid on its top.

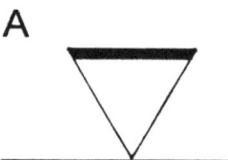

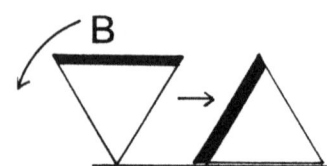

If a vertical line from the center of gravity falls exactly through the point of support, the pyramid is in a stable balance.

A minute force can change the position of the pyramid if by only a hair's breadth and our pyramid topples over, as it is now off balance.

In conclusion, note that any external force needed to change the balance from stable to unstable or off is directly proportionate to the size and shape of the base of support. The smaller the base of support, the less energy is needed to shift the center of gravity. Or, if you like, the narrower the base, the more sensitive the balance to any outside influence. In equestrian language, we would call these outside influences influencing balance the weight aids.

off balance

new stable balance

Gravity and Balance

Let's take these theoretical concepts of balance a step further and apply them to ourselves. Two simple experiments will demonstrate the concept's validity as you experience for yourself how it feels to be in a stable balance or an off balance.

1. Take a wide stance and ask a friend to: a) push you laterally off balance.	1. Take a narrow stance and ask a friend to: a) push you off balance laterally.

There's no way she can do that, is there?	It's very easy, isn't it?
b) push you longitudinally off balance. This is quite easy.	b) push you longitudinally off balance. This is very easy, too.
2. Now take a wide stance and raise your left leg off the ground. You will topple to the left unless you catch yourself. From stable balance to off balance in a fraction of a second.	2. Take a narrow stance and raise your left leg off the ground. You will stay upright without even noticing the minute adjustment required to keep your center of gravity over the solid base. This is stable balance to stable balance.

3. Take a wide stance, with your legs wide apart and jog or run for 200 feet (the length of a diagonal in the dressage arena), while maintaining a wide stance. See how it feels, looks and performs. Terrible, right?

3. Take a narrow stance and sprint the 200 feet (or diagonal of the dressage arena). It will feel effortless and you might even qualify for the Olympic Team in the next games!

IN CONCLUSION

The wider the stance, the more pedestrian the gaits or strides. Think about it: there is a reverse relationship between stability and the freedom of movement. You are very safe and stable on a large base, but you get into trouble when moving. The opposite is when you are in a narrow and delicate balance, but easily able to move.

This is something to remember when we apply it to the horse or ourselves: a moving human as well as a moving horse always compromises between these extremes, each to his own best feeling or training. Or, to put it differently, we have an opposite relationship between the safety of a broad base and the need to compensate the balance for every step or movement, or that of a narrow base with a more precarious balance but requiring minimal compensation and adjustment at every stride, where it is much easier to initiate and maintain movements.

With the horse, the center of gravity is not absolutely fixed and can change according to the position and carriage of the horse within a very limited range.

On a horse at rest and standing square, the vertical line from the center of gravity is always closer to the front legs, while the center location depends somewhat on the conformation and the base of support of the horse. However, this changes during the horse's movement and also within the different gaits.

The next sections assume that the reader has at least a general understanding of the biomechanics of the horse. I will not go deeply into those topics here since extensive literature is already available, but I encourage all serious riders to educate themselves on biomechanics.

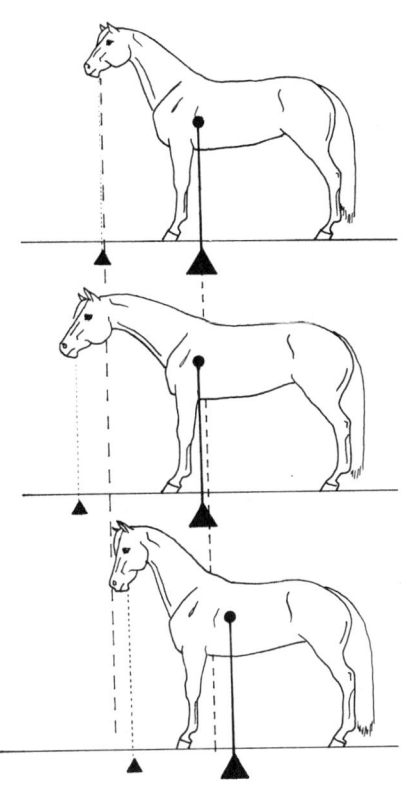

THE HALT

Let's now apply these concepts of stability and balance to a horse standing at rest.

The basic conformation of the horse in relation to his balance consists of a relatively large steady mass at the given height above the base, containing the center of gravity as well as the center of mass. Attached to it in front, but not supported in any way from the ground, completely outside the base of support, and exceedingly mobile is a "balancing pole" weighing

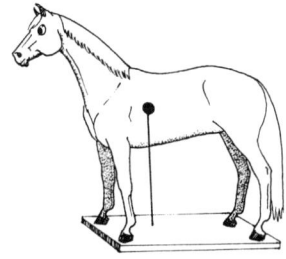

approximately 150 to 250 pounds; this is the head and neck of the horse.

THE LATERAL VIEW

At this position, the center of mass is in the chest, about halfway between the sternum and the spine, which is the same location as the center of gravity. The vertical line falls within the base of support.

The "balancing pole," that is, the head and neck, are in a neutral position. If the horse is slightly crooked to the left or right, there is a little bit more weight on the legs on that side.

THE VERTICAL VIEW

Looked at from this view, we can see immediately that the center of gravity has an ample space in front and in back of it, 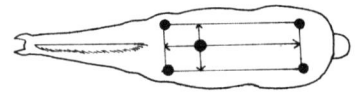 only reaching the limits of the base of support under very unusual circumstances. And note that, perhaps even more importantly, it has less or little space to move laterally.

The more narrow the stance, the more delicate the lateral balance becomes. At rest, it clearly does not matter how wide or narrow, or how long or short the base is, since nothing moves, and the only objective is to counteract the pull of gravity with the center of gravity confined within the base of support.

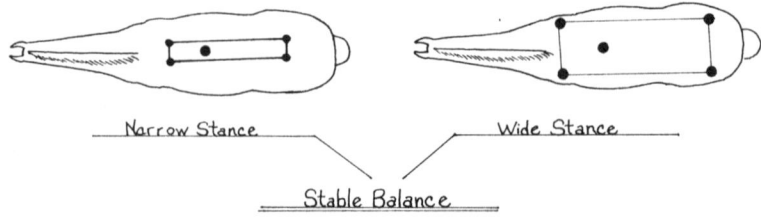

The following two horses Ahlerich and Prinz Eugen are very narrow and perfectly balanced under their respective riders. Then compare with the photo of Entertainer.

World champion Ahlerich in 1985 in Copenhagen: the salute at the end of the Grand Prix Special.

A great American horse with an amateur rider

GRAVITY AND BALANCE   17

A naturally wide stance: safe and solid but not for gaits and elegance. Michael Klimke on Entertainer.

In the trot and the counter-canter, Prinz Eugen remains perfectly balanced under his rider.

The Walk

Now let's move on to the walk, a gait in which each limb moves with the three others remaining on the ground: left hind/ left front/ right hind/ right front, for example.

What happens to the base of the support when one leg is lifted up? The base of support is cut in half, which then puts the center of gravity in an unsteady or off balance position. The horse has no choice but to move the center of gravity into the remaining 50% smaller base of support which changes its triangular configuration with every step.

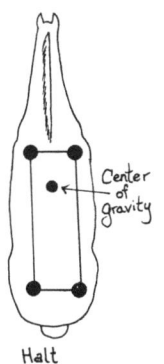
Halt

This is accomplished by a dual mechanism which you can observe by watching a horse walk with or without the rider, either from the front or from the back. One part of the mechanism is in the front, and the other is in the back.

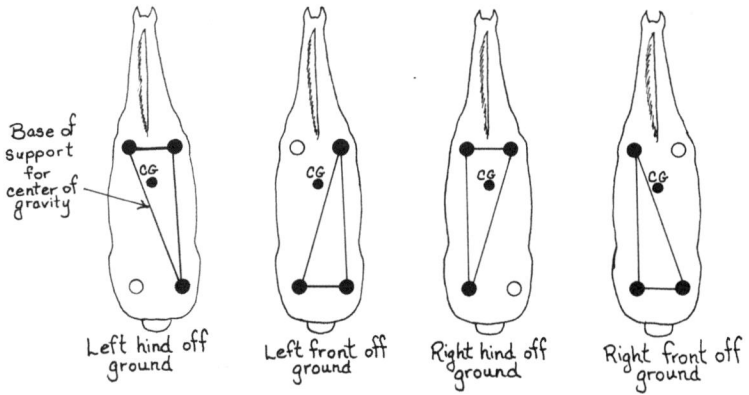

Base of support for center of gravity

Left hind off ground   Left front off ground   Right hind off ground   Right front off ground

The narrower the horse moves, the less compensation is needed. Therefore, the better will be its balance. Also, while the configuration of the base changes its shape, the horse moves steadily forward, maintaining its center of gravity, well supported.

So what are the mechanisms the horse uses to maintain his balance?

When, for example, the horse lifts the left front leg, removing the support for approximately 300 lbs., the horse swings (if allowed to do so by the rider) his head and neck. This laterally shifts 200 to 300 lbs, more or less, back into the base of support, while at the same time he nods his head up and down, reinforcing this balancing action.

When a horse lifts a hind leg off the ground, the support of the corresponding hip vanishes and the hip sinks down, and 200 to 300 lbs. or more are no longer supported. The spine then rotates a little bit, the abdomen swings to the other side, displacing again between 200 to 300 lbs. toward the base of support. The horse is then maintaining the center of gravity within the 50% remaining of the base.

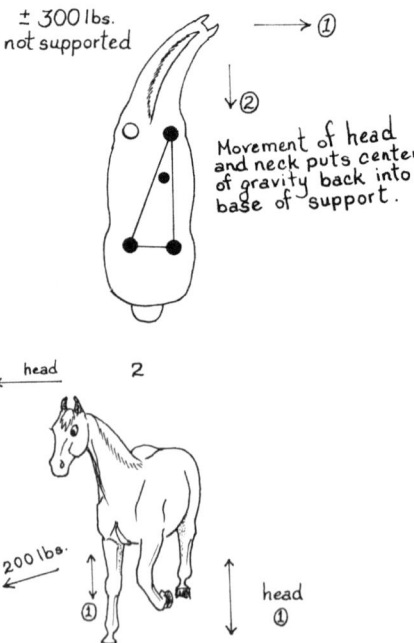

This rotation of the horse's body in shifting the weight is only possible because the horse's body is suspended in a muscular sling between the front legs which is not attached to the skeleton or the thoracic cage by a clavicle as, for example, in humans.

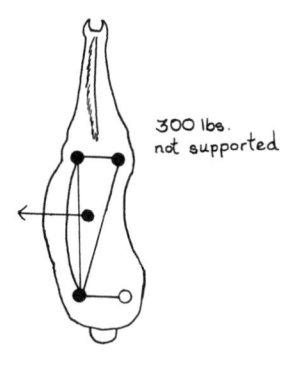

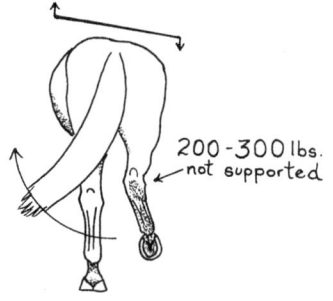

What should be noticed is that these corrections occur sequentially and not simultaneously. So, when sitting on your horse, you can feel that the changes of seat and leg are not coordinated with the tugging on the reins made by the movement of the head and neck.

This fact was recognized and addressed a long time ago by Seunig, who recommended that in the forward transition from the halt, as the horse lifts one front leg that he be given the liberty to balance himself with his head and neck by the rider opening the fingers of both hands. Otherwise, the horse will fall in toward the side on which he takes the first step.

Again, as previously discussed, the narrower the base of support the less correction is needed for balance and the easier it is to convert supporting power into pushing power on a straight line. The wider the base, the more adjustment is needed and less energy can be used to step forward. This is the same as we saw in the human example given earlier.

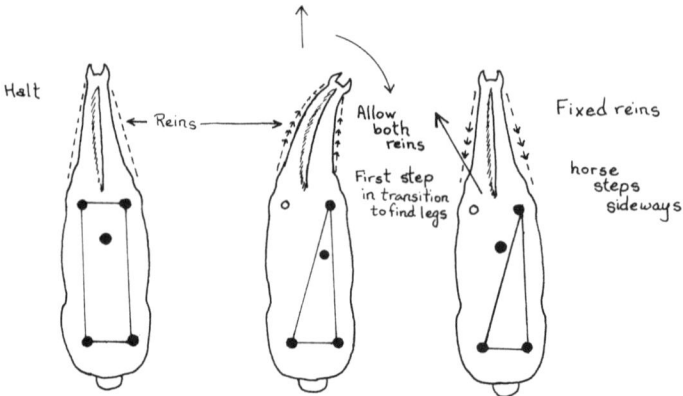

This mechanism also explains the development of pacing when the rider tries to collect the walk from the front, and thereby prevents the balancing mechanism of head and neck for the front legs by too much rein action. This leaves the horse only the second mechanism, the swinging of the belly from left to right, to keep his balance.

The result is that the front leg has to adjust to the rhythm of the hind leg and as the horse cannot or is not allowed to compensate with his head and neck for the movement of the front leg in the correct footfall, and so the horse paces.

This was recognized even as far back as the 16th century, if not longer. As we can see in some of the old manuscripts, horses were deliberately taught to move in a diagonal walk, with the right hind and left front together, as in the trot. This was done in order to maintain balance and to not have to compensate for the changing of the base. This walk is not practiced anymore today and is very difficult to achieve. However, under natural conditions in the rein back, where the horse is much more insecure, he immediately and automatically will take the diagonal strides. According to the rules of both the FEI and the

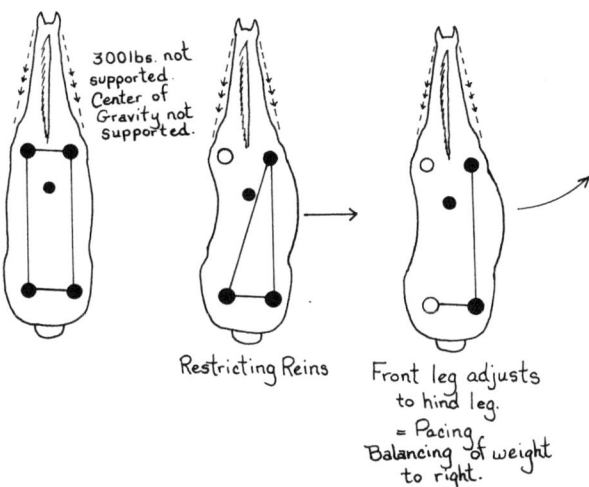

AHSA, these are the correct footfalls for rein back but not for riding forward!

Therefore, horses that go wide (plus other factors of conformation) will develop pacing more easily than those that go more narrowly because they need more compensation in lifting the front legs and so are more susceptible to interference from poor hands.

This explains why the walk is the most difficult gait and the one most easily disturbed by the rider. Most riders do not understand it, but when I see a horse pacing, the first question I'd like to ask is, why did you let this happen? And now that he does it, why don't you fix it? Unfortunately, many riders and instructors can't give an intelligent answer or correct advice. To reinforce this statement, just read the statement on the walk in the FEI and AHSA manuals.

It is at the pace of the walk that the imperfections of dressage are most evident. This is also the reason why a horse should not be asked to walk "on the bit" at the early stages of his training. A too precip-

itated collection will not only spoil the collected walk, but the medium and the extended walk as well.

—from the **FEI *Rules for Dressage Events*, 20th Edition** and **AHSA 2000 *Rule Book***

THE TROT

Next let's look at the trot. We have already looked at the problem of the forward transition from the halt and the necessity for the horse to compensate for the first step, which are identical in walk and trot.

But then things change dramatically. The footfall in trot is diagonal: left hind with right front, then right hind with left front, totally synchronized. The fact that two diagonal legs are off the ground together balances out the loss of support, and always bisects the center of gravity with the opposite diagonal which is still on the ground.

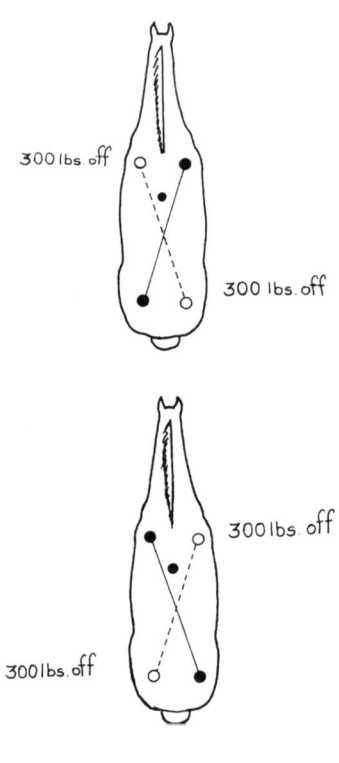

The effect on the center of gravity is totally predictable. One diagonal line of support always bisects the center of gravity so it is continuously supported, and needs no adjustment to a new base. It is like a little pyramid turned upside down, and rather delicate to any outside interference, such as weight aids.

Remember, the more narrow "the gait," the more potential to orient the energy forward.

No wonder the trot is the basic gait for dressage training; there is no need for the horse to relocate his position at every step as in the walk. Since the base is very narrow where the diagonals cross right under the center of gravity, it is extremely sensitive to outside influences such as any change of position of the rider as when changing direction.

This fact was recognized centuries ago and is today reflected in this theorem from the German Dressage Federation that no horse can really extend or collect unless it moves on a narrow track. It is even better if the hind legs do not only move forward, but also inward, toward the center of gravity (from **Advanced Techniques of Riding**, the German National Equestrian Federation).

Now, looking at the trot half pass, we know that up until about 15 years ago, horses were kept almost straight with only a positioning of the head at the poll. Excessive bending in the direction of the movement was not recommended, a fact that is today reflected in the FEI Rule Book which suggests that the flexion in the half pass is less than in the shoulder-in.

By putting too much flexion of the head and neck in the direction of the half pass, we add 200 to 300 pounds of additional weight on the leading front leg, and so throw the equilibrium off base. Instead of being light, up and forward, this position causes the leading front leg to be weighed down and, as we often see, leads to an irregularity of the footfall in front. See the illustration on the next page.

Now a horse that goes wide is very good for a beginner with no steady seat or position, but its gaits are not destined for true achievement in dressage. We also often see a horse that normally goes narrow begin to go wide behind when pushed for-

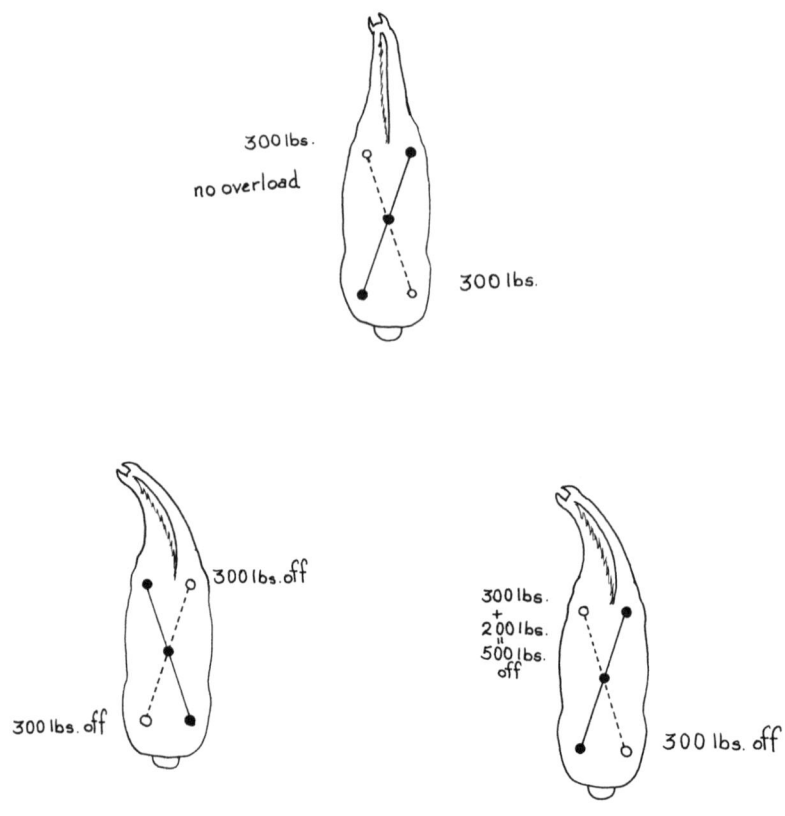

Not balanced

ward too much into an extension in the trot as the horse feels insecure and enlarges the base of support. An otherwise narrow horse going wide in the medium or extended trot is a clear indication of having asked too much too soon. For this reason, many trainers develop the medium and extended trot on a circle where the footfall prevents the horse from going wide behind, and both hind legs step under at every stride.

In dressage, we use expressions such as "shift more weight onto the haunches." But how can we, or for that matter a horse, shift weight backward if the body remains the same, with

GRAVITY AND BALANCE

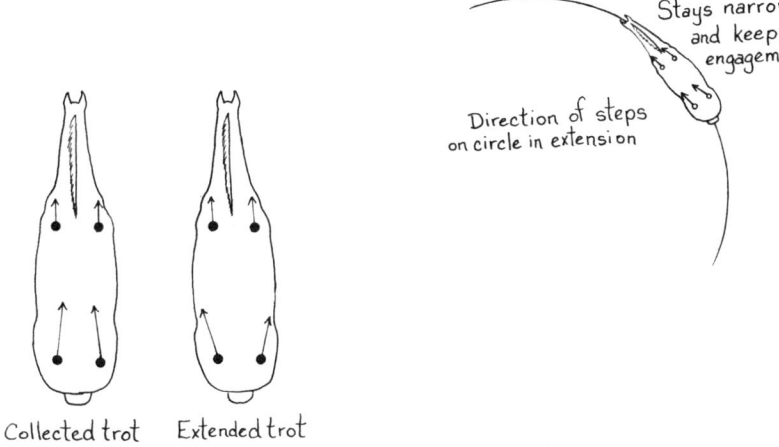

Collected trot   Extended trot

neither the center of gravity or the center of mass changing its location significantly?

While the general idea is correct, what happens in reality is different. The center of gravity stays, but with the hind legs moving further forward and under the horse, the base of support shortens in the back. As a result, some of the mass is now behind the position of support, acting as the balance over the hind leg.

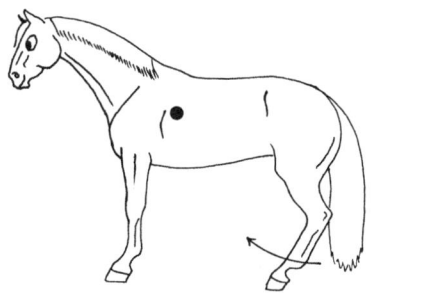
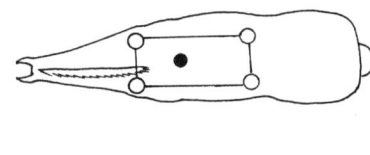

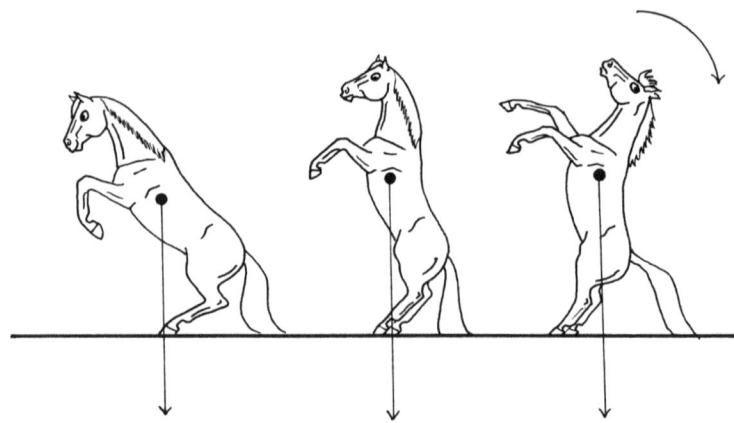

Now, if we keep pushing this trend farther and to the extreme, we find ourselves executing the classical movements *levade* and *courbette*. And interestingly, in these movements, even though they may have originated from a narrow piaffe, the horse will widen his stance and broaden the base of support. But never push your luck so far that the center of gravity exceeds the narrow base of the hind legs where they touch the ground or you will topple over backwards!

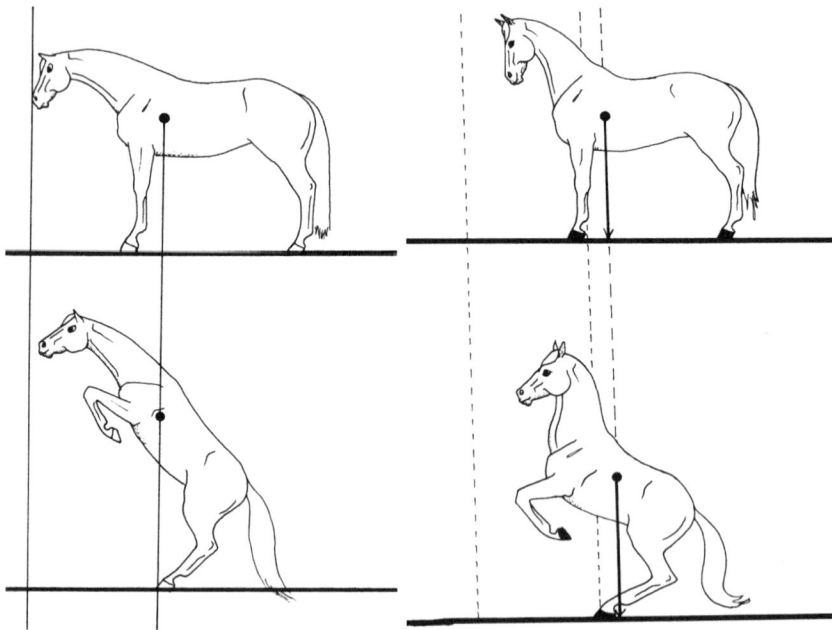

A vertical line from the center of gravity gets closer and closer to the hind legs where they touch the ground.

The Canter

In the canter, the horse faces a completely different situation from the walk or trot when we analyze it in relation to balance and the center of gravity.

First, the canter is a diagonal movement from the outside rear to the inside front, as opposed to straight forward.

Once on the leading front leg, the horse must balance himself backward, to the outside rear leg, by using his head and neck. As this happens during the phase of suspension and allows the horse to reorganize for the next stride, it is at this exact moment that the rider, by giving with an allowing inside hand, can assist the horse in the rebalancing from the inside front to outside rear by giving the horse the freedom to use his head and neck.

In the canter, neither the outside rear nor the inside front can directly support the center of gravity. The only support of the center of gravity at the canter is the diagonal with the simultaneous footfall of the inside hind and the outside front.

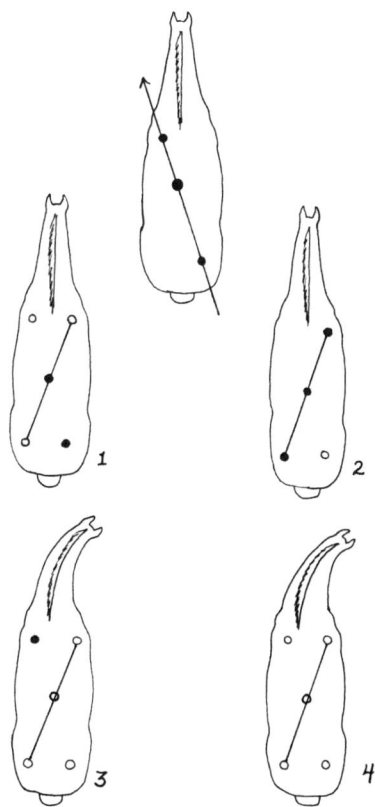

The motion is basically that the horse rolls over this diagonal, from the outside hind to the inside front. Even though the canter seems to be the gait with the most motion, the centers of gravity and of mass are relatively stable and the action is either behind or in front of them.

The problem for the horse is coming back from the front inside to the rear outside; this is when the horse must have his balancing pole, his head and neck, and be able to throw his head to the outside and up, as done in freedom.

So you can see that in riding and positioning the horse in the direction of movement, we make it difficult for the horse. This is why every serious author, past and present, insists on a soft inside hand to allow this movement.

Based on this consideration, it is clear that the more the horse canters on the forehand, the bigger the effort that will be required to relocate and re-engage the rear hind leg. Therefore, this horse will need even more freedom of the head and neck to rebalance itself. Then as the horse becomes progressively more and more collected and consistently under himself behind, this allowance of a soft rein becomes less and less important. However, it will always exist. There is a debate over whether or not the horse in canter, particularly in collected canter, can truly be absolutely quiet with his head and neck carriage, or if a minimum of this movement is still required at a collected canter to maintain a consistent and safe support for the center of gravity.

So, looking at the horse's gaits from the perspective of gravity and balance will give us insight in the basic kinetics. This examination of the kinetics clearly shows that only the leg or legs that do not support the center of gravity can be influenced by our leg aids, which explains immediately why timing is the key to effectiveness, not force. Remember also that the more narrow the horse moves naturally, the better its natural balance but the more sensitive it is to leg and weight aids.

We see that all movements of the horse are coordinated to keep the center of gravity supported and that these movements are limited by the biomechanical limitation of the skeletal structure and the muscular system.

Fear develops if and when the horse anticipates that these functions are threatened, leading, for example, to resistance and refusal in front of a cross country jump, or balking at unfamiliar, disturbing, new dressage movements. Training should therefore consist of developing the potential of reflexes and reactions within the limits of these two constraining factors, gravity and biomechanics, and progressively educating the horse to handle the limits of its possibilities with confidence. Using force is always wrong and is an indication of a lack of understanding of the rider. The use of force is often induced by the rider making unreasonable demands on the horse and thereby becoming frustrated—not very fair or attractive!

To conclude, when riding we must respect the need for balance on the horse's part, or we will otherwise create resistance, evasion or even refusal.

CHAPTER 2

TIMING

Once we understand how the horse keeps his center of gravity supported on a base formed by a given configuration of his legs as determined by the gait, we can understand how important it is that we as riders respect this basic function of balance. Any interference with this situation leads to a disturbance of the horse's balance and, as a consequence, resistance or avoidance of our aids by the horse.

In all gaits, there are always one or more legs not involved in the mechanism of balance to keep the center of gravity supported. And it is this leg or legs which most easily respond to our leg or rein aids as they are free to move and respond.

You can try this out yourself. Just stand on one leg, which carries all your weight, and use the other leg to kick it out. It won't budge an inch. But the moment you take the weight off this leg and stand on the other one, you can move it in any direction you desire. It is exactly the same with the horse: you can only affect or influence the leg of the horse that carries no weight. This happens when the leg moves off the ground and reaches forward.

So, the effectiveness of leg aids is not in the strength in which they're given or in the spurs, but in the *timing*. If you have timing, you don't need spurs. This is the basis of the old saying that spurs must be earned; they should be only allowed once a confirmed seat has been established and the correct timing of hands and seat and legs has been achieved. It is indeed a sad sight to see so many lower level riders poking their horses with their enormous spurs without having the slightest idea of what they are doing, and totally out of synchronization with the gait they are trying to ride.

Let's look, for example, at the walk. Based on what was said earlier, remember that the center of gravity is always supported by a triangular base which constantly changes each time the horse moves one leg forward. Looking first at the movement of the hind legs, we see that the weight-carrying leg alternates from left to right to left, while the opposite leg moves off the ground reaching forward, and does not provide a base for the center of gravity or balance. Therefore, the only hind leg that we can influence with our leg aids is the one moving off the ground and reaching forward.

The influence of our lower leg pressing gently on the side of the horse causes a muscle contraction that pulls the hind leg more forward. This, however, ceases the moment the horse puts the foot on the ground, and there is nothing we can do until the same sequence repeats itself. Any rider with some feel in his seat knows exactly when this happens as the same side of the horse lowers itself as the leg reaches forward. The key to effectiveness is not so much the pressing with our calf, but stopping the pressure when the leg touches the ground until it again steps forward. The key to a good walk is the ability to wait for the right moment.

The same sequence repeats itself on the other side and, as a consequence, our aids must shift accordingly from left to right to left—and not be applied simultaneously.

Therefore, "activating the hind leg" is not done by banging away with both of our legs but, instead, alternating our support in the rhythm of the kinetics of the gait. Using both legs simultaneously often interferes with a good walk due to that muscle contraction mentioned above, which, when incorrectly applied, prevents the weight-carrying leg from really pushing well forward, and in doing so reduces the length of the stride.

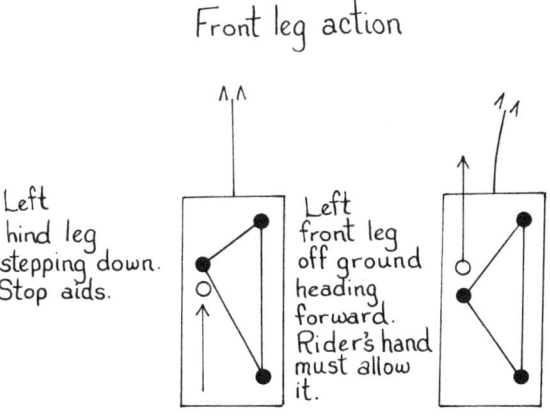

There is another consideration in the walk (unless it is a free walk on loose reins). In the medium, extended and, above all, collected walk, we should maintain a contact which, by the definition from the old Masters, should be soft and allowing. Why?

Looking at the horse's footfall, we see that when the hind leg reaches out and touches the ground at the most forward point, the entire front, shoulder, leg and neck of the horse stretch forward on the same side. Insofar as we control what's happening in front of our seat through the reins, we must allow this to happen freely if we want the best walk the horse is capable of.

Therefore, in our aids, we must consider the front and the back of the horse. In order to allow the horse to do this reaching and use his neck and head to maintain his center of gravity over the shifting triangular base, we must allow some freedom by slightly opening our fingers. If you don't have a feel for it, just look down and coordinate the opening and closing of your fingers with the horse's shoulders moving forward or coming back.

You should note that the leg aids and the allowing with the reins are not really concurrent, but sequential. But as many riders are poorly coordinated, it is acceptable to open and close

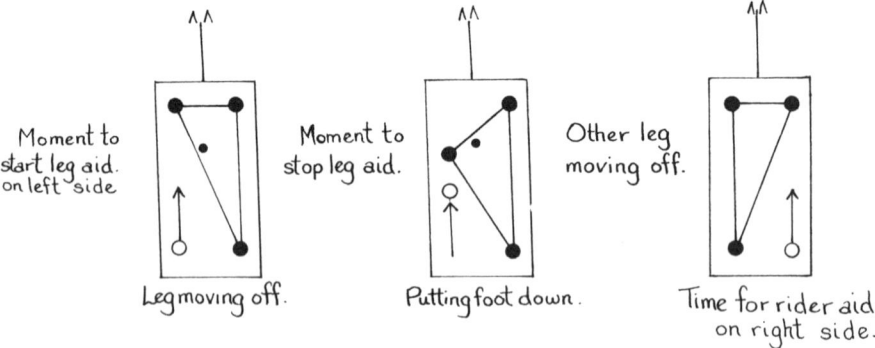

our fingers slightly in the same rhythm as we use our alternating leg aids.

Looking at the kinetics of the walk from the point of view of the center of gravity and its support, it is clear why the front of the horse, if not allowed to follow the natural balancing, will fall back on the rhythm of his haunches and the horse will pace. Furthermore, since we humans are not ambidextrous and are usually stronger on the right side, the extent of the lateral walk is often not the same to the left and right in pacing horses.

As for the trot, we have noted previously that it is the most balanced gait and, due to the alternating diagonal support, very responsive to the leg aids. But, again, the response comes only if our timing is coordinated with the leg we want to influence as it comes off the ground, reaches forward and carries no weight. It is also the gait where, for the first time, we begin lateral movements such as the shoulder-in, renvers, travers and half pass. All of these lateral movements require either the inside or outside leg of the horse to cross over or step under toward the center of gravity. As a result, the timing of our leg aids becomes absolutely essential to initiate and maintain these movements. By now the rider should be sufficiently educated so that he or she can feel which leg is coming off the ground. If not, this lack of education becomes immediately apparent by the rider's uncoordinated action or constant banging of the inside or outside leg, (or, even worse, both), totally unrelated to rhythm the hind leg of the horse we want to affect. A good example is the shoulder-in.

The key to the shoulder-in is our effort on the inside hind leg, where the difficulty is not so much to apply the leg aid at the right time, but to wait patiently for the correct moment to repeat the aid over and over with rhythm of the gaits. This also

Shoulder-in left

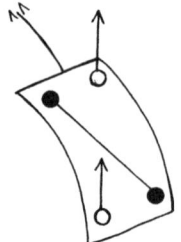

Inside hind, outside front reaching forward. Time for leg aid.

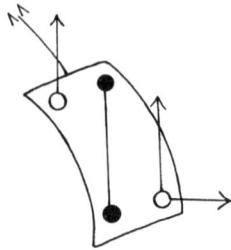

Contain outside leg to prevent stepping out when leaving ground = alternating leg aids.

applies to the renvers, travers and half pass where we must coordinate the timing of our leg aids to the fraction of a second when the outside hind leg can be influenced to step forward and across. These leg aids must be coordinated with a correct seat and weight distribution of the rider in addition to the position of the hands, which will be discussed in the chapter on weight aids.

Considering the canter, we face a totally different situation, one not encountered in normal human locomotion. The canter is also quite different from the walk or trot of the horse. The gait is diagonal and not symmetrical, and starts from the outside hind leg rolling over the diagonal of the inside hind and outside front, and finishes on the leading front leg, while stretching the entire inside forward, and then balancing the mass back on the outside hind leg.

Our aids must therefore follow the same diagonal pattern by first encouraging the outside hind to step under to push off, followed immediately with the aids on the inside to step forward. We then allow, through our giving inside hand, the leading front leg to reach forward. Once this front leg is on the ground, we allow the horse a little freedom in the head and neck to balance himself back to the outside hind.

The sequence and application of the aids goes completely against human kinetics, but horses are so kind in trying to please that often totally illogical techniques have results. We will talk about the canter more in a later chapter.

In conclusion, the common factor in all the gaits is that the kinetics of the horse dictates the correct timing of our aids. Further, the key to good riding is the development of feel, which allows us to integrate correctly into the movement of the horse and apply our aids effectively when the horse is capable of responding. Essentially, this is what is meant by *timing*.

CHAPTER 3

THE CENTER OF MASS

Consideration of the center of gravity explains a lot of matters in the movement of the horse. But in order to understand it fully, we have to introduce the concept of the center of mass. This is because riding is, fundamentally, the motion, movements, gaits and transitions of a relatively large and heavy body.

The center of mass has the identical location as the center of gravity, but represents a completely different concept. The center of mass is always present, irrespective of the location of the body, whereas the center of gravity does not exist, for instance, in outer space where there is no gravitational pull. Nevertheless, the body of the object is still the same.

According to Newton's Laws, the center of mass acts in opposition to any force of acceleration or deceleration. Therefore, it is fundamentally involved in all up and down transitions in riding. A practical example exists when we start or accelerate our car and are pushed back into the seat. Then, if a driver crashes into a telephone pole, you know what happens: he or she is thrown forward into the airbag or held by the seatbelt.

As to velocity, another Law of Newton states, it is a time rate of change of position. Or, to make it perhaps more clear, velocity is the time rate, or speed, in a given direction.

Then, the power needed to achieve a certain velocity up or down depends on the weight of the object, represented by the center of mass of the body, and how fast the change has to be accomplished. Further, that when all forces acting on a body are balanced, there is no unbalancing force, and the body either remains at rest or continues to move in the same direction with constant velocity.

What this means is that in a halt or a steady forward motion, the center of mass is neutralized and therefore not influencing the state of affairs. However, the center of mass becomes a dominant influence opposing any change in the steady state if it is executed in, say, an up or down transition or in a turn. This should make it immediately clear that in order to maintain a steady state in either motion or at a halt, little effort is required. On the other hand, to increase or decrease the velocity up or down when in motion or into motion from a halt requires much more power, depending on the rapidity with which the change has to be affected and the weight that has to be influenced.

A typical example is that when accelerating the car from 0 to 60 miles per hour, the time required depends on how much you step on the gas, but while cruising along at 60 miles per hour only a fraction of the initial power is needed.

The Center of Mass

This theoretical consideration also can be demonstrated with a very mundane exercise which some of us do everyday: mucking out stalls and then pushing the wheelbarrow up and down the manure pile! Really, how much more basic can you get? But it exemplifies exactly what we have been saying.

Looking at the full wheelbarrow:

1. at rest,

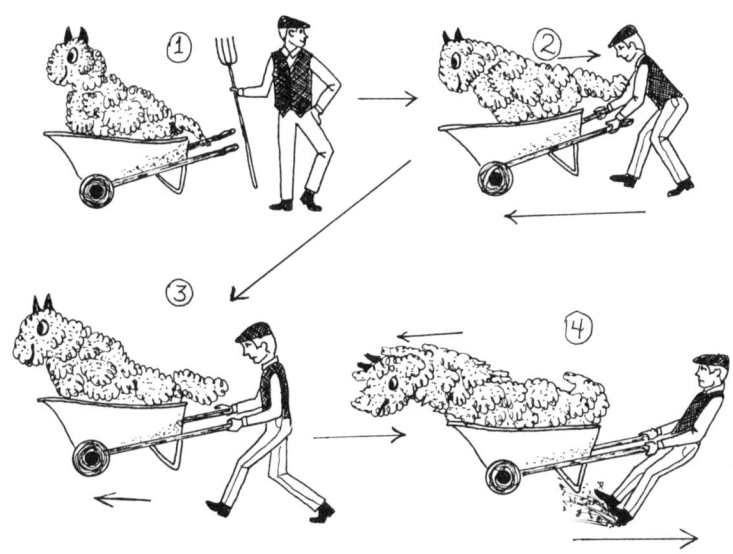

2. getting it moving,
3. continuing the movement, and
4. stopping the forward motion when needed.

The above represents a situation when the power affecting the center of mass is always in the back, the same as you hope to ultimately accomplish in a well-made, collected horse.

1. At Rest
There is no opposition by the center of mass to change.

2. Getting it Moving
In starting up towards achieving a steady velocity, the effort required depends on the weight and, consequently, the opposition of the center of mass to the change of the status quo.

3. Continuing the Movement
In this phase, there is no opposition from center of mass. The velocity keeps steady.

4. STOPPING

To reduce the velocity to zero by braking, we must overcome the opposition of the center of mass which tends to keep pushing forward.

Applying this concept to the horse at a halt, or in the initiation of a forward gait from the halt, or in an increase in velocity within a gait, or from one gait to another, it is identical to what we see with the wheelbarrow. The push forward comes from behind, opposed by the center of mass.

On the other hand, when slowing down or coming to a halt, thereby reducing the velocity of the movement and the forward thrust of the center of mass, the horse has two options: either brace against the center of mass and its thrust with the front legs, or stop the thrust from behind by holding back with the haunches planted under his body.

This makes for the difference between a down transition on the forehand (often referred to as "off balance") or a correct transition from an engaged hind leg, where the horse lowers the croup and brakes from behind. Another important practical conclusion from this analysis is that just riding forward with an unchanging velocity does little or nothing to strengthen the horse's haunches or develop the proper response to correct aids. On the other hand, riding transitions up and down within a

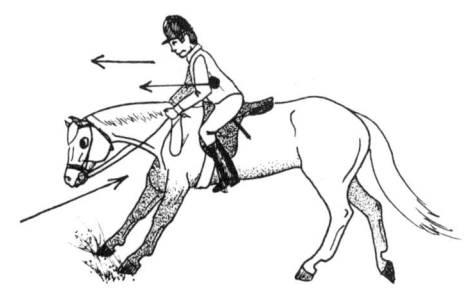

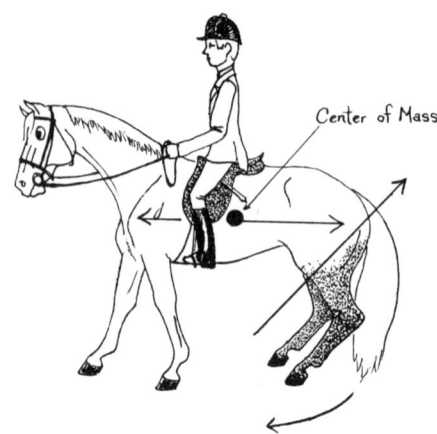

gait, or from gait to gait, leads to a complete control of the center of mass from behind. This requirement becomes more and more important as you move up the scale of competitive dressage. In fact, the mastery of the center of mass from behind is a decisive factor in all the FEI level tests.

STOPPING ON THE FOREHAND

STOPPING FROM HAUNCHES

The center of gravity and the center of mass are inseparably connected as can be seen in the following examples:

1. The horse's center of mass is stopped abruptly from the front.

2. The rider's center of mass is unopposed, taking him over the fence (even when in such a situation the rider must maintain a correct position according to George Morris!).

3. But, when the center of gravity is no longer supported in order to maintain the status quo, gravitational pull will bring the rider back to earth and into a new stable balance, stopping the center of mass as well. The rider can now be considered to be again in a steady state, though certainly unwillingly.

Assessing the effect of the center of mass on riding, we note immediately that the centers of mass of horse and rider are independent of each other and often move differently from each other, sometimes quite suddenly. Fundamentally, a fall occurs when the center of mass continues in its same direction, preventing the center of gravity from remaining over its base of support. The fall is almost always in the opposite direction of the movement of the horse. That means that if the horse jumps to the right, you fall off to the left, if a horse stops in front, you go over his head, and if a horse takes off under you, you fall backward and roll over his rump. The basic mischiefs in riding lie in the action and the center of mass as we will see later on in more detail, but most people do not realize it.

An example demonstrating this principle is the following. If you drive your car down the highway at 70 mph and want to make a turn to go in the other direction, you must slow down to 2 or 3 mph. Otherwise, the velocity and the mass of the car would spin you out of control.

Similarity, if you want to ride a correct pirouette, the key is to first reduce the velocity of horse and rider to one canter stride on the spot, and then ride the pirouette forward with correct weight aids. The problem and difficulty is in the approach, not in the pirouette.

The Center of Mass

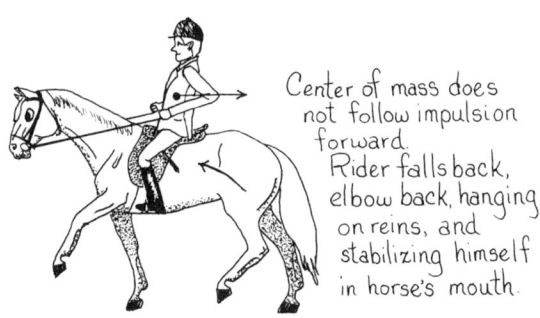

Center of mass does not follow impulsion forward. Rider falls back, elbow back, hanging on reins, and stabilizing himself in horse's mouth.

The beginner rider in particular has not yet learned how to "go with" the horse, which is nothing other than anticipating a change in velocity and compensating for its effect before it happens. This is only possible after the rider has developed a seat that stays with the motion of the horse and can compensate for the change of impulsion and the center of mass so as to prevent the center of gravity from interfering. As long as the seat leaves the saddle at every stride, particularly at the sitting trot and canter and sometimes even in the walk, if the pelvis does not follow the pivoting from left to right of the horse, the center of mass becomes dominant over the position of the rider.

Once the rider is "in the air," with the seat out of the saddle, there is nothing to hold the rider in position. The natural reflex when the horse moves forward under the rider is to grab the next available item, in this case the reins. The rider steadies himself using the horse's mouth, opposing the effect of the center of mass which is not following the impulsion of the horse.

This is best demonstrated in the transition to the canter from the sitting trot or walk. The horse pushes off from behind, accelerating his center of mass forward into a more forward state of velocity. The rider's center of mass stays behind and even the center of gravity often falls behind the base of support, that is, the rider's seat. This necessitates the rider hanging onto the reins in order not to be left behind. This is further aggravated by the human reflex to move the elbow and arm back when the hips go forward as you will see in the chapter of human kinetics. The rider not only steadies himself with the mouth of the horse, but actually yanks the bit backward. No wonder then so many horses refuse to canter with a beginner.

What I often hear in a clinic is that a horse leans on the rider and is heavy in the rider's hands. But, if you look closely, it is the rider who hangs on the horse's mouth. We humans have been programmed for so long to use our arms and hands for stability, for instance, since we learned to crawl and walk as babies that we are simply not aware of it. Until we make a very conscious effort to understand the problem, it will be difficult to change.

This is also the basis of the old saying that spurs have to be earned by a good seat and good hands. In the early days of civilian dressage, we had many outstanding European judges, and one made the following comment: In my country, nobody is allowed spurs unless the instructors allowed it, but here in the USA, the size of the spurs worn in the lower level is in direct relation to the incompetence of the rider. If they knew how to ride, they would never have to use them on the lovely horses you have here."

What should be taught first is what an allowing inside hand is, and the technique to properly compensate and anticipate the contrary action of the center of mass. This is done by leaning forward slightly and receiving the same push of forward impulsion from the horse's haunches as the horse's center of the mass does. This will then prevent the arm from being pulled back when the hip goes forward because the rider has fallen behind the motion. Otherwise, if the center of gravity of the rider is pushed behind the horse's motion by the center of mass, the rider is thus dragged along by the horse and will hang on the reins, instead of moving with the animal. So, in the correct canter depart, not only must we anticipate the push from behind and prevent this from happening by anticipating the effect of the center of mass, we also allow the inside hand to go slightly forward, allowing the horses to stretch into the new lead.

Clearly, we have here several basic factors that work against us in learning to ride properly. Now this same problem, though to a lesser extent, may be seen when the horse moves to extend in the trot. The rider falls behind the movement and the thrust coming from the haunches, then hangs on the rein and never lets the impulsion go through. This problem is clearly addressed by the FEI rules that suggest that, in medium and extended gaits, the horse be allowed a longer and lower frame with the head in front of the vertical. This comes from so-called "allowing hands." This also leads to a rider's position that is slightly forward, since riding behind the vertical has nothing to do with the driving or forward aids and is consistently an interference for the proper movement of the horse.

So, when we are trying to ride correctly, we must establish a harmony between the center of gravity of the horse and the center of gravity of the rider in a combined new location. This is while, at the same time, anticipating and compensating for the antagonistic effects of the center of mass.

And, we must adjust our human kinetics and movement to those of the horse so as not to interfere. Otherwise, our actions can not be called aids anymore and become strictly interferences.

No matter how well we understand this in principle, it is a completely different matter once we are on horseback. But if you realize the importance of this dynamic and strive to accomplish it, you will be much faster in making progress than riders who have no idea what is actually going on and must wait for years and years until—maybe—someday their body naturally adjusts without them even knowing what is going on.

Remember, the center of mass of the rider always wants to do the opposite of what the horse and rider have decided on! And a good part of what we call *feel* is simply anticipating and compensating for this fact. Staying balanced on our horses, with both centers of gravity (ours and the horse's) properly aligned, is only possible if we learn to anticipate and control the effect of the center of mass.

CHAPTER 4

THE ORIGIN OF BIOKINETICS AND THE CENTRAL NERVOUS SYSTEM

The movements of the horse are limited by the range of motion of the skeletal joints, based on their anatomical construction, and cannot go beyond it. Within these limitations, movements are executed by antagonistic muscle groups. Antagonistic muscle groups exert opposite movements. One group may bend the joint and the other stretches it out, putting the first muscle group back in a state where it can contract again. The one exception is the range of the horse's front legs, which are not connected to the rest of the skeleton.

But on their own, muscles, joints and the skeletal structure cannot act. If medically there is a paralysis, such as after an accident, with a complete loss of muscular activity, it is the nervous connectors to these muscles or muscle groups that are interrupted without any change to the muscles themselves. So muscles and joints are only the "end" organs, executing input but unable to act on their own.

As for the muscles of the skeletal system, they can only contract. Their strength depends on the efficiency of the energy metabolism and the number of muscle fibers involved. This can only be improved slowly and pushing conditioning too fast or repeating the same movement over and over again usually leads to damage, pain, resistance and the evasion of the correct movement. The stretching of the muscles back to their original position so they can contract again when asked to do so is accomplished through the antagonistic muscles, gravity or any outside force. Muscles cannot stretch themselves, only contract.

So the question then arises: what maintains motion and balance? The answer is the central nervous system, or CNS. It regulates and activates the entire musculoskeletal system. Therefore, balance is orchestrated and produced in the central nervous system and not in the peripheral muscular skeletal apparatus.

Let's examine the central nervous system and, simplifying greatly, we must first realize that animals including humans operate on two levels. There is the *cortex*, which is the outer layer of the brain, and the location of our voluntary decision-making as well as our conscious sensory perception. But only a small percentage of all incoming impulses reach the level of consciousness, and very few specific commands to muscles originate there.

The far more complex process as far as movements are concerned take place in the *subcortical layers*, where incoming impulses automatically trigger appropriate responses, called reflexes, on a continuous, uninterrupted basis. It's like the working of a properly programmed computer (no Y2K problems!). This structure also contains the vestibular apparatus, part of the inner ear, that records position and movement. This apparatus is fundamental in establishing the balance of the human and horse, and orchestrates the fine-tuning of the neurological impulses emanating to the muscles. As a matter of fact, humans as well as horses have no basic awareness of actively guiding the muscles that keep us upright or moving and in balance, or in coordinating motions. All we do is decide to do something, and these subcortical centers do all the rest of the work. Only if balance and equilibrium become unstable and disturbed does the cortex take notice or interfere by creating local reactions to correct the situation as quickly as possible.

The *peripheral nervous system*, leading from the central nervous system to and from the end organs, is a simple conducting system, namely, the direct communication to and from the muscles and joints. Without a doubt, the *afferent*, or sensitive nerves, are the ones most important since they relay to the central nervous system a continuous flow of information concerning our posture, pressure in the articulation and tone of the muscles, the pull of gravity: in short, a complete picture of the body in its environmental space.

The *efferent* nervous system or the nerves leading to the individual muscle fibers from the subcortical centers are rather uncomplicated, and just send the impulses decided upon by this center directly to the muscles.

The key to any movement, gait, position or action is the connection from the afferent to the efferent nerves, creating reflexes independent from the cortex or consciousness or any voluntary decision. These neurological connections and pathways leading to the reflexes are not inherited but are established after birth until the end of puberty when the ability to establish new reflexes ceases. However, establishing such reflexes and interneuron connections takes time, consistency and repetition. This is where the feeling for and the reflexes to maintain balance become gradually established. This is also where the real training of the horse, as well as for humans, takes place, and not in the build up of muscles, which is generally referred to as conditioning.

These facts are by no means limited to riding. We know, for example, that children can learn any language. An American learns Cantonese and Mandarin without a problem as the Chinese child in New York learns English. But if later in life, you want to learn a new language, your laringual, tongue and lip muscles simply will not be able to adjust to the new pronunciation and you will always have an accent.

A female gymnast beginning her training at three or four will have her best years around puberty. However, once she develops a feminine body configuration with a different weight distribution, her abilities are no longer than same, as her highly defined reflexes no longer reflect the facts. On the other hand, male athletes do not have this problem as their bodies do not change so dramatically and their best performance years are usually in their late 20s or early 30s.

We all have the same CNS muscle and skeleton, and we all use only a fraction of its potential. Just decide to do a backward somersault—maybe it's better that you don't even try! Yet you have the same body as a circus artist who easily does somersaults.

Our reflex patterns are only geared to what we do in our daily lives, but this is not the end of it. While we expect the horse to be absolutely straight and ambidextrous, we are all one-sided, mostly right, and have created a world and environment to suit us and our reflexes. Just look at cars, where everything of importance—like the gear shift—is on the right side, and the left is just along for the ride.

This domineering right-sidedness was even recognized by the Duke of Newcastle, who lived 1593 to 1676, in his book on horsemanship. He devoted a whole chapter recommending that the reins be held in the left hand only, which is softer and less domineering. This was required by old AHSA and FEI tests for some movements but was abolished by the FEI for the 1972 Olympics. Even so, it truly demonstrated if the rider was skilled and the horse properly trained.

This is not the end of our human limitations either. Even though we have enormous input from our peripheral receptors, we all have an inaccurate perception of ourselves, how we react, look and present ourselves in the environment around us. This is well demonstrated when looking for the first time at a video of ourselves on horseback, which is always a very sobering experience. For that reason, videos often give us a better grasp of our limitations then the endless, repetitive comments from our trainers.

A baby takes one to three years to learn to walk, run and stay upright, even though it was born with the complete central nervous system. However, the baby did not have reflexes at birth. This also explains why we all move somewhat differently as nobody grows up identically to anyone else. And, as we noted before, we also know that unless you begin to train a child when he or she is four to five years old, the child is unlikely to become a top gymnast, skater, skier, ballet dancer, or tennis player. The older child or adult will not have the same advantage in developing the intricate reflexes of coordination needed for these sports and in maintaining the balance and body coordination. After puberty, once you are grown up, you can not learn any new reflexes. What you must do instead is try to connect or rearrange those you already have to satisfy new demands if you start an activity different from the one you exercised during your growing period.

It is an entirely different matter to teach adults to ride who have never been on a horse and will have to make do with whatever neurological connection they have, or to teach children who can progressively build up specific reflexes and are coordinated and adjusted to riding while they are in the growing up stage. This is why it is most sensible to develop the neurological synapses and reflexes during the horse's developing years, and physical fitness and conditioning only after the joints are consolidated. This helps prevent the joints from being damaged by excessive demands by the muscles.

Just "muscling up" a horse for the sake of building muscles is senseless. It often causes an early breakdown and infirmity of the horse as the joints, tendons and skeleton are not yet matured and become progressively damaged, terminating the career of the horse in his prime. This is the key to developing a sound horse that lasts for over 20 years and does not break down.

Remember, when you train a horse, you never train the muscles or joints to execute movements, but you create the reflexes and the neurological impulses that guide the muscles. Muscles on their own are useless. It is the central nervous system that requires the most training.

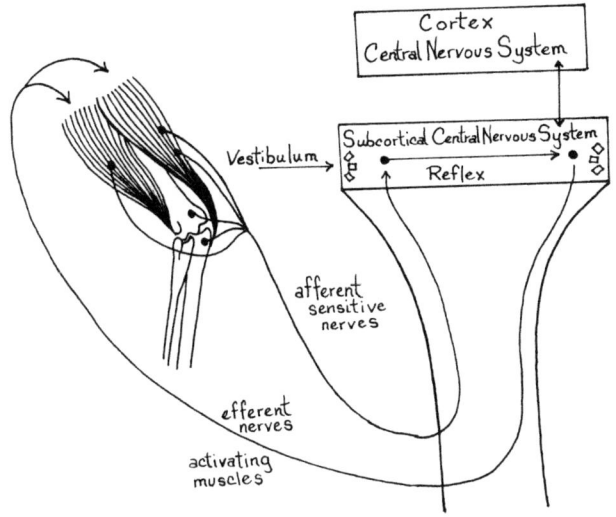

From this point of view, it makes a lot of sense that the old Masters preferred to school a horse twice a day, for 15 to 20 minutes, instead of 45 minutes as we do. By doing so, trainers then were able to reinforce the correct reflexes without getting the horse tired or excessively muscled up.

Consider this from François Robichon de la Guérinière, writing in 1729:

Many horses are put under saddle much too young, resulting in incurable damage to their backs and haunches since, due to their not yet completed development they are not yet capable to accommodate safely the requirements made on them. The age at which Dressage should be started in a Warmblood horse depends on the climatic conditions of his geographic area of upbringing and is six or seven years of age, and under certain circumstances eight years.

This leads us to the simple conclusion that, just as with the young horse, the beginner rider simply cannot use his muscles as suggested by the instructor, since he does not yet have the reflexes needed. So, the instructor should progressively reinforce the correct reflexes and, eventually, the rest will fall into place as the reflexes develop.

I should also point out the danger of developing incorrect reflexes, which leads to problems. And, the longer they exist, the more difficult they are to eradicate and substitute with correct reactions.

Now an inexperienced human who climbs on horseback has only one resource to stay there: using those reflexes he has for his kinetics to stay balanced on his own feet. But this resource simply does not fit the three gaits of the horse. So, the very first objective in teaching a beginner should be to develop systematically the reflexes that suit the movements and gaits of the horse.

To develop correct new equestrian reflexes, we must first learn to listen to the input of our own sensory receptors of joints, muscles, skin and eyes, for example, and in particular the seat, since we first must learn to be aware of what happens under us before we try to influence it. This input originates in the muscles used in the motion of the horse, and are the basis of developing the correct equestrian response reaction and reflexes.

The fact that we all have the same muscles and nerves does not necessitate that we can do all the movements we wish, but only those for which we have developed reflexes over many years. That takes lots and lots of time.

Humans use only a minute fraction of all potential movements, the limitations being the reflexes and coordination of our subcortical centers.

CHAPTER 5

HUMAN KINETICS

BASED ON GRAVITY & CENTER OF MASS
IN RELATION TO BALANCE

As we discussed in the first part of this book, human kinetics changed dramatically once man adopted an upright position 3 ½ million years ago. The base of support for the center of gravity diminished dramatically to the area covered by the feet. The center of gravity itself moved much higher up on the body. As a result, all automatic reflexes developed with only one objective: to keep the body in balance.

Man relied on his brains and the ability to use his arms for tools and weapons. Locomotion was reduced to one gait, mainly one foot after another, with a significant reduction of speed. The ability to escape or pursue prey on foot was lost, replaced by the use of the brain. All other mobile parts of the body were also integrated in this reflex system, with a relatively stable area from where all movements originate, that is, the pelvic structure, which is itself quite rigid. The human way of moving was greatly simplified in comparison to horses, or other four-legged animals who depend on speed and agility for survival, which was no longer the case for man.

Those reflexes required to maintain our balance develop in the first part of our lives when babies first begin to crawl. Early on, when babies try to stand upright, they fall forward or backward. As they progress, it becomes easier and easier to stand up for a while.

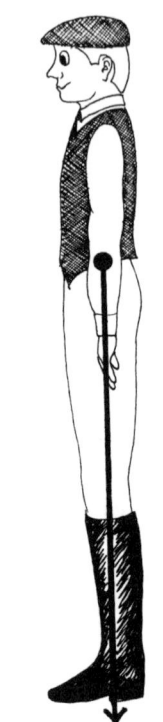

When we stand up, we are unconscious of how we do it, what muscles we are using or how to influence them. Whenever we do something physical, we are basically out of the picture consciously. Just stand up from a sitting position and ask yourself, how did I do that? Try to analyze what muscles are involved in standing up, and then, once you are balanced on your two feet, what the difference is in the tone of the musculoskeletal system that keeps you in the balanced position. Don't be surprised if you have no idea. This fact has been long recognized by kinesiologists and particularly in the work of Moshe Feldenkrais and others.

The problem in riding is that we take all of these human reflexes, even though we have no control over them, over to the horse, who operates on totally different principles of kinetics. The typical example of the human inability to control our muscles for equestrian requirements is the rider who is just being put on a horse, whose legs are constantly banging uncontrollably, who is out of balance and hanging on the reins. This new rider is completely unable to follow any of the teacher's instructions and admonitions to "keep the legs quiet, sit up and stay in balance." The rider is frustratingly unable to do anything about it no matter how hard he tries, even though he has exactly the same muscles and nerves as an advanced rider.

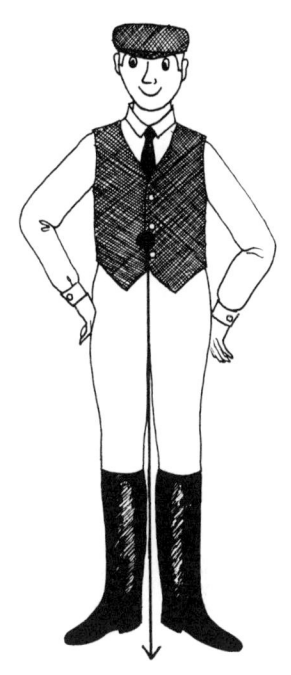

Good riding is, therefore, the progression to, and the painfully slow introduction of, entirely new reflexes that are in harmony with the horse. These new reflexes must supersede our human balance reflexes for when we stand on our feet. At first this is done by a conscious effort, step-by-step, but ultimately becomes automatic after years of correct riding. Then the rider can be said to have developed *feel*. A good rider actually has two reflex systems: one for when standing on his feet and one for when sitting in the saddle.

Understanding these facts will help the progressive transformation from a beginner to a rider with feel, but it will not shorten the time required. It just points out those areas where we must concentrate in order to get in harmony with the horse.

Remember, it takes a baby, who has all the needed brain cells, nerves and muscles, at least two to three years to start walking, running and playing. We cannot expect to be any faster when we try to develop an entirely new kinetic system for riding.

So let's look at the human way of moving which is very simple in comparison to the horse's way of moving. Both, of course, must maintain balance, but that is where the similarity ends.

1. In humans, the center of gravity is high above the base of support, much higher than in the horse.

2. The base of support in our human body is very small, compared to the large surface outlined by the horse's four legs. The center of gravity in our case must be centered above the two feet we have on the floor.

3. As a result, any movement or change of position requires instant compensation as there is no leeway or tolerance for a mistake.

4. There are three basic compensatory mechanisms if the center of gravity moves outside the base of support or very close to its edge. Consider the following example:

>a. Shift one leg in a new supporting position and then lift it up.

>b. Use your arms, upper body and head as a compensatory mechanism, throwing it to the other side.

>c. Grab anything within reach with your hands and pull or support your upper body back into balance. This is obviously what happens with the reflex to grab the reins and steady the upper body using the horse's mouth.

In the case of walking, (which incidentally has the same footfall as running), the following takes place when we swing the leg forward: the center of gravity is moved forward, outside the base of support. If nothing else happens now, the human will just fall forward on his nose as he is off balance. However, this is counteracted by:

1. Putting the shoulder of the same side back and down and letting the arm swing backward.

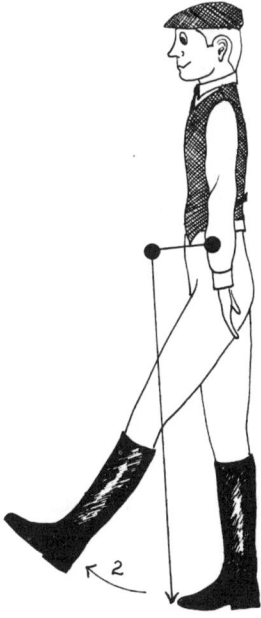

2. Shifting the center of gravity to the leg remaining on the ground. This is achieved by contracting the opposite abdominal muscle and pulling the pelvis up on the side that the leg is moving forward.

The hips rotate forward and upward while the shoulder and arm on the same side move back and down. This is the basic

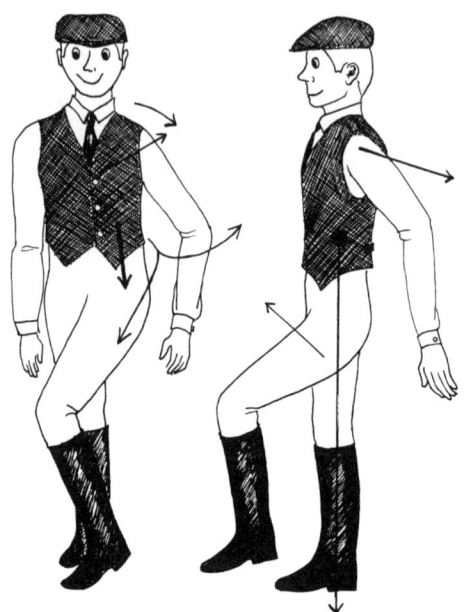

reflex ingrained in us from the time we take the first step after crawling around on four limbs. Again, it is completely unconscious and difficult to change once we've become accustomed to this movement.

The throwing of the shoulders and arms back as the hip of the same side goes forward, that is, this certain torsion between the shoulder and the pelvis, is also the basis of many riding problems. It leads to what we so often see in beginners, those contradictory aids when the seat and legs try to urge the horse on into the canter, while the shoulder and arm move back, preventing it. It is not that we can do much about it instantly, but recognizing the problem is the first step in carefully and deliberately working on it. This way we can actually solve the problem, instead of just getting frustrated and hoping that one day it may correct itself.

THE ROLE OF CONFORMATION

Beyond these basics, what also determines our kinetics, or the way we move, is our individual body build, or what we could call human conformation. This varies enormously and influences the way we keep ourselves balanced.

Our human conformation ranges from long, slender bodies with long legs to those who are top heavy with short legs. There are people who are very heavy from the middle down, and very light on top, and just about any variation in between you can think of. Therefore, the mechanism to keep balanced is highly individualized and never the same for two people. Forcing these various conformations into a standardized frame on horseback makes no sense; in teaching riding we must individualize just as much as nature has.

In the cavalries of old, only men with a predetermined body build were accepted, including in the Spanish Riding School, so that a standardized teaching approach could be followed.

The difficulty in harmonizing our body movements is demonstrated in even such select groups as the Rockettes of Radio City Music Hall, or the marching of the parade battalion of the old German and Russian infantries. It takes months and years of training to achieve the precision of these groups. This is due to the fact that even while very similar, each of the individuals in these groups must modify his way to a given standard which is not his own.

The infinite differences in movement also explain why we can recognize a friend even at a considerable distance from behind when he's walking in a crowd.

SHOCK ABSORPTION

Another factor fundamental to human kinetics is our design for shock absorption. It takes place in the lower limbs, using the articulation of the ankles, knees and thighs to amortize the impact, while the upper body and the arms assure balance. The pelvis remains the steady centered structure connecting the

HUMAN KINETICS

Compensatory Mechanism
- Shoulder and arm rotate and swing back on same side.
- Hip and leg move forward opposite rotating movement to keep center of gravity over supporting leg.
- Opposite shoulder and arm move slightly forward to shift weight onto supporting leg.

mobile upper and lower parts of our body. In comparison with the horse, he has no such mechanics operating in him. This is very visible when seeing a horse go over a jump.

If you observe a skiing competition over moguls, you see the total adjustment to the dips and moguls are made with the legs, while the center of gravity and the pelvis are kept as even as possible during the entire course.

However, in riding, the situation is totally different in that the solid, unarticulated center part of our body is the one that must adjust to all the movements and impacts of the horse. The legs are not part of this mechanism when we sit in the saddle.

No wonder the hunter rider two-point position is preferred by many riders, or for example, the rising trot, as the weight and movements are absorbed by the mechanism of "impact management" and not so much the seat.

Shock Absorption

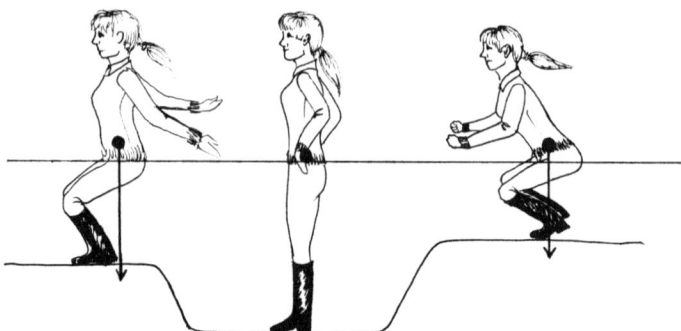

The articulation of the lower limbs and the position of the spine act like springs or the shocks in a car while the pelvis and center of gravity remain steady.

Humans on a Horse

The pelvis, which has no springs and no articulation, is basically quite rigid. It must absorb the swinging motions of the horse; if not, it leads to bouncing. The more this part of the body is kept rigid, the more the rider will bounce.

The Circus Artist

Standing on the rump of the horse can use human reflexes for balance. This is a piece of cake compared to sitting an extended trot. On the other hand, the effect of the center of mass is accentuated.

Although our famous McClay junior equestrian riders are marvelous over fences and in a rising trot, when you ask them to sit the trot, you'll often see a sorry picture of sour faces and unhappy horses.

We do not develop under nonequestrian circumstances a mechanism to absorb motion or shocks with our pelvic structure. If you lose balance, for instance, in skating and fall on your rear-end, it is with a thud and not with a bounce. It is a shock through the spine and, literally, is a real pain in the rear end for a while. This is really a very crucial difference that we will examine later.

As we've previously noted, the inventory of movement that we perform in our daily lives is basically very limited and highly routine, tailored to our living habits. In reality, it is only a small fraction of what our body could theoretically accomplish.

Just try a leap into the air like the great Nureyev, or a somersault like a gymnast (if you are smart, you won't even try!). You have the same muscles, nerves, vestibular functions, subcortical and cortical central nervous system, and you may make the conscious decision to do so, but that is the end of it; there is no mechanism for transforming the wish into reality.

The same thing happens when you sit on a horse, and your teacher tells you to keep your legs quiet, and not to bang them around. No matter how hard you try, there is nothing you can do to stop it, as we discussed in the chapter of the central nervous system. In some ways, we are prisoners of our own nervous system.

Right- or Left-Handed?

The next fundamental fact of human kinetics is that we are not ambidextrous. An experienced clinician sees immediately if his riding pupil is left- or right-handed. This preference not only affects the hands and arms, but the whole body. How do we expect the horse to be absolutely straight, and equally supple to the left or right, if our own influences on him are not the same to our left or right? What is even worse is that we are not even conscious of this fact.

In addition, horses are not ambidextrous either and are always different to the left or to the right. Our own one-sidedness may help to correct it a little bit or make it worse.

Further, when we look at the alignment of the human spine, we not only have different bends in the *lordosis* and *kyptoses*, but most of us have some degree of scoliosis which does not help our position on horseback or the symmetry of our weight aids. Would you buy a horse that has such a back? Probably not.

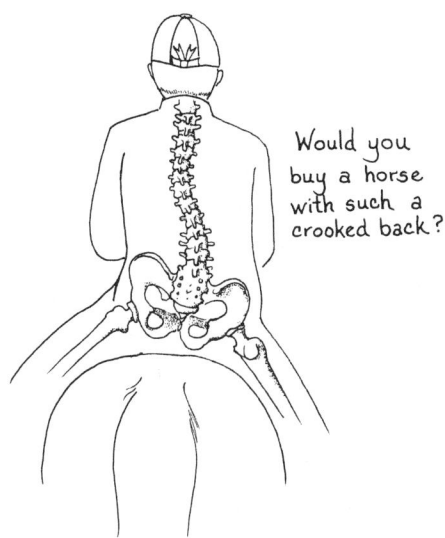

Looking at these facts, one easily comes to the conclusion that we humans are a pretty sorry species when it comes to physical attributes!

THE ROLE OF THE PELVIS

In addition to these factors above, there is another fundamental difference in kinetics when we climb on horseback. Under normal circumstances, such as when we walk, the pelvis is the anchor or solid, stable part of our body around which our lower limbs and upper body and arms move.

On horseback, it is the pelvis that is the main contact with the perpetually changing base, and the upper body, arms and legs are supposed to be quiet. This is exactly the opposite of what we are doing when we are not on horseback. Furthermore, the center of gravity must be supported and centered above the pelvis, not the feet. The effect of the center of mass must be compensated for, not by the feet, but by the position of our pelvis in relation to our upper body.

Ideally, from the basis of the constantly shifting pelvis, we must develop movements with our legs on an absolutely independent basis, left or right, that we would ordinarily never need or use. And our right-handed supremacy needs to disappear, in favor of a completely even, independent use or our right and left hands, and our arms and legs.

An example is the action of the legs of a beginner in the rising trot, which are properly timed and coordinated with the lifting and forward motion of the hind leg. But once this rider sits down, he starts banging with both legs, totally out of synchronization with the movement of the horse, even though, as far as the horse is concerned, it is the same gait.

For this reason, some European instructors prefer to teach lateral movements such as shoulder-in, *renvers*, *travers* and half pass in the rising trot, selecting the diagonal that is relative to the hind leg of the horse that we want to influence. Long ago, Richard Wätjen told me that there is no right or wrong diagonal, but that it all depends on which hind leg you want to affect. The important thing is that your leg is totally synchronized with the hind leg's leaving of the ground and reaching forward, as discussed in the chapter on timing.

Once your seat, however, is truly confirmed, this does not matter anymore as your leg aids are in harmony with the movement of the horse and his hind legs. Without a correct, sensitive seat, you will never be able to fine tune your aids, and achieve the proper timing for the movements you want to ride. This obviously is a constant struggle for the beginner.

Another fundamental difference from standing on our feet as compared with riding, is the origin of the incoming impulses related to our position in space. Normally, it is the sensory receptors of our legs and feet, together with our dominating visual perceptions and the vestibular center, that maintain us in balance when standing or moving. But in riding, it is the sensory receptors of our seat and thighs that try to signal to the brain what is going on.

Initially, however, this is without the slightest success because there are not yet receptors or reflex mechanisms to take advantage of these incoming impulses. This is because we never used these parts before we climbed on horseback; we just did not use our bodies this way.

With time, however, such connections are established. We learn to feel exactly where each leg of the horse is placed in all three gaits and to make the adjustment and muscle coordination to maintain the center of gravity. We learn to anticipate the effect of the center of mass, leading to corrections as needed. Once this has become absolutely automatic, we can say that the rider has developed *feel*. The old saying that you know what feel is when you get it, while correct, only proves that most riders don't really know on what it is based.

The key to this picture is the fact that in human movements the pelvis is the central steady point for upper body, arms, and legs to move freely.

In riding, the pelvis follows all the motion of the horse and the upper body is supposed to be steady and quiet, same as the hands, arms, and legs.

CHAPTER 6

HUMAN BIOMECHANICS AND THE SEAT

If we want to become absolutely ambidextrous, that is, capable of moving our arms, hands, legs, and body independently from each other, we must have a solid center. What makes this so difficult in riding is that the base is not steady and still, but is always moving.

Recommendations on how to sit properly on the horse go all the way back to Xenophon (430 B.C.-354 B.C.), and all subsequent authors. Almost all of them, down through the centuries, were made based on the personal experience of the authors, mostly by men, for men.

However, in the USA, particularly in the sport of dressage, women make up more than 90% of all equestrians. There is a fundamental difference in the pelvic anatomy which has not

really been taken into consideration so far for either an effective seat or an appropriate saddle. To me, though, understanding the basics of the seat based on human anatomy and the differences of biomechanics between males and females is essential to teaching or judging dressage.

To summarize the problem briefly, there are two contradictory requirements for the pelvis. The first is *stability* so the rest of the body can use it as a base to keep the center of gravity in place and compensate for the effects of the center of mass, allowing independent hand and leg aids. The second requirement is *mobility* to follow the movement of the horse.

In addition to the gender differences, everyone must develop his or her own individual seat, and the struggle to do so was the same 10,000 years ago as it is today. Besides the variety of seats described in the literature in the last 200 years, look at the pictures of riders in international competitions, such as the

Olympic Games or the World Equestrian Games, and you will see that no two riders sit alike. Compare Dr. Reiner Klimke with Christine Stückelberger or Christilot Boylen. You cannot say that these riders cannot sit or are ineffective. But why this enormous variation?

Any combination of horse and rider necessitates a series of compromises and adjustments, and since the horse has to do the physical work, the primary responsibility for adjustment rests with the rider.

With the following lists, I would like to bring attention to some of the aspects of the seat used in dressage that I find are often overlooked. Here are a few basic facts:

1. No object can stay balanced on a moving base if only supported by one or two points.

2. The minimum support base must therefore be three points or more.

3. The kinetics of a moving horse can only vary within a limited range but are consistent for each gait. Remember, too, that humans only have one gait.

4. The saddle, if properly adjusted, is positioned between horse and rider, and is capable of transmitting the movements of the horse to the rider and those of the rider to the horse. This obviously requires the saddle to fit both the horse and rider (difficult with mass-produced, unisex saddles). While many of the varied types of saddle pads protect the horse's back through their thickness or shock-absorption capabilities, they can also remove the rider's influence by making his seat aids nonexistent. The rider sits above the horse, not with him.

5. We must also consider whether it is a male or female rider who is trying to maintain balance on a narrow base of support while simultaneously communicating with the horse.

Male and female bodies have distinctive constructions which affect riding but also vary widely within a group. This is not a new discovery: Sioux Indians made different saddles for women and men to ride in.

Starting with the basic concept that one cannot be secure if supported only by one or two points, we can now look at a male and female pelvis to see how each gender might find stability.

THE MALE PELVIS

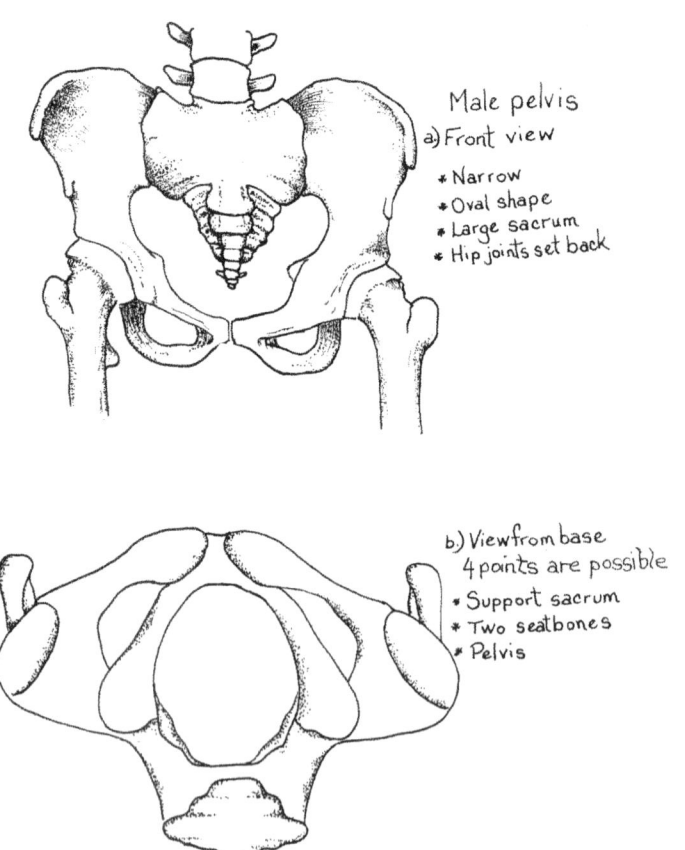

Male pelvis
a) Front view
* Narrow
* Oval shape
* Large sacrum
* Hip joints set back

b.) View from base
   4 points are possible
* Support sacrum
* Two seatbones
* Pelvis

The illustrations show the male pelvis as seen from the front and bottom. Several observations concerning the male pelvis:

1. The male pelvis is rather narrow and more oval than the female, and is smaller and enclosed behind by a large, solid sacrum, which has some mobility.

2. The hip sockets are set somewhat back outside the seat bone (ischium) and are in the axis of the pelvis.

3. The entire structure can pivot back and forth from the lower spine, including a certain freedom to pivot left and right. But the lordosis, or hollowing of the back, is always less than in women.

4. The most forward, solid point is the pubis or crotch. The most backward point is the tip of the sacrum. Compared to the female pelvis, the male sacrum is compact, in a more vertical position, and closes the pelvic structure from behind.

5. The arch of the pubic juncture is narrow.

Looking at the male pelvis from below, we see:

1. The narrow oval shape.

2. The thigh bones are fixed in the axis of balance of the spine. This allows for two seats: the two seat bones and the pubis or crotch, and the two seat bones and the sacrum if the seat is tucked under and the rider is in a rather slouched position.

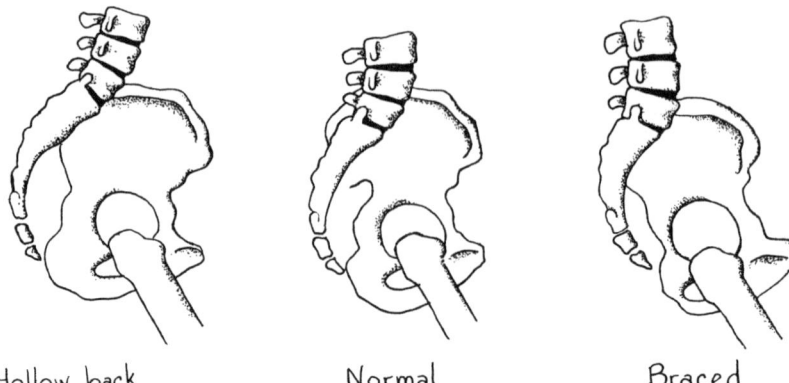

Hollow back   Normal   Braced

Even though all of these points are not on the same inclination or plane, both triangles can be used for sitting in a secure way. So, the male seat has four potential points of support. If a man braces his back and creates a lordosis, the crotch lowers. Then the two seat bones and the crotch become the supporting triangle on the saddle. But by tightening the abdominal muscles and forcing the pelvis into a slouching position with the seat under him, the triangle of support becomes the two seat bones and the sacrum.

The sockets of the thigh bones are under the spine in the dressage seat. Due to their lateral position on the pelvis and the less angulation inward when compared with women's, the thighs can easily stretch without having the toes point to the outside. Furthermore, in males there is a flat construction of the inner thigh that helps in maintaining a leg position that is flat on the saddle, with the toes pointed forward and the heels away from the horse. The ligaments that attach the thigh to the pelvis do not pitch the male rider forward as they do in the female rider.

THE FEMALE PELVIS

Now let's take a look at the female pelvis as illustrated. Note that:

1. The pelvis opening, or birth canal, is wider and rounder than in the male, and the pubic arch is wider.

2. The sacrum is small, shorter and positioned backward and not downward: it does not close the opening at the back of the pelvis as in men.

3. This, together with a fixed lower lumbar vertebral column in a lordosis, or hollowed back, reduces or nearly eliminates mobility backward.

4. This configuration allows for only one triangle to sit on, namely the crotch and the two seat bones, since the sacrum is so small and placed back and up from the seat bones.

5. The lordosis and position of the pelvis pitches a woman forward, onto the pubis, just the opposite of the position of men.

6. The thigh bones and hip sockets are not under the vertical axis of the spine but are much more forward, pointing more inward since the pelvis is much broader. Combined with round thighs, this forces a rotation when in the saddle, and the toes go out while the heel and the spurs go in. The lower leg and knee are away from the saddle, making them ineffective.

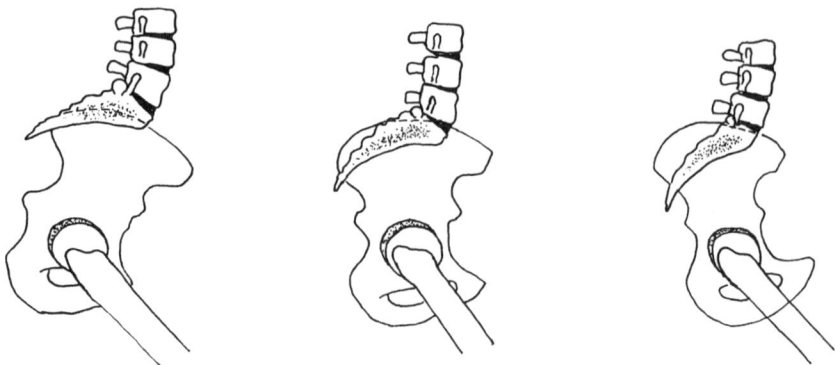

Lateral view of female pelvis in different seat positions

7. The arch of the pelvic juncture is wider and if pushed down on a narrow saddle, the pressure is absorbed by the soft tissues of the crotch, not the bony structure, which can become very painful.

8. The hip joint ligament, different from in men, pitches the pelvis forward and accentuates the lordosis when the legs are stretched down and rotated outward.

This situation is further aggravated by the stretching down in attempting the long, low dressage leg, a position which actually pivots a woman away from the saddle. The ligaments affecting the movement of the thigh in its socket do not allow lengthening of the leg without causing some more lordosis in the lower back, and the loss of flexibility and shock absorption in a woman, something that does not happen in men.

The anatomical correction for a good seat, therefore, is different for a woman than for a man, depending on the extent of

Human Biomechanics and the Seat

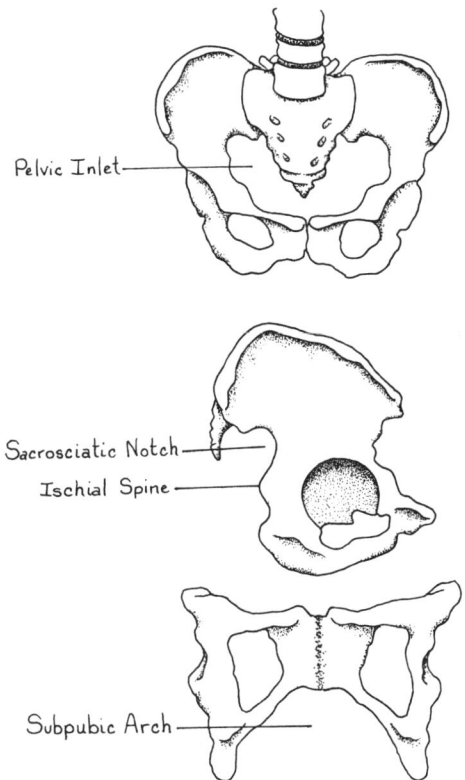

each individual's differences. Women with slender, male-like pelvic position and structure have much less trouble adopting the "standard" seat than those with a more feminine body type. The female body type simply does not allow for the "standard" seat in many instances, since pushing the leg down rotates the pelvis onto the crotch and exaggerates the lordosis, while eliminating and suppressing any swing and elasticity, and turning the feet out.

To correct and help women to achieve an effective seat, which is not necessarily the standard dressage seat, the following must be considered:

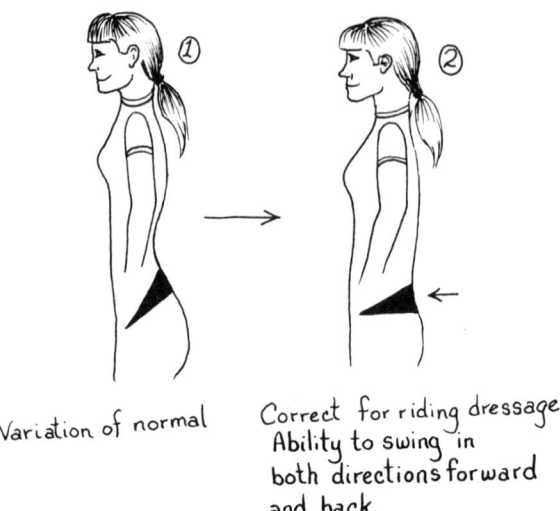

Variation of normal

Correct for riding dressage Ability to swing in both directions forward and back.

1. The lordosis must be eliminated, and the suppleness and ability to swing off the lower spine reestablished by moving it from the extreme lordosis to a more vertical position.

2. Depending on the conformation of the thighs, the female rider should be allowed a less-straight leg than a male, with more angulation of the thigh and knee. This helps by bringing the seat bones down and the pubis up, thereby preventing the pitching forward onto the crotch with no solid support. It also diminishes the outward rotation of the leg.

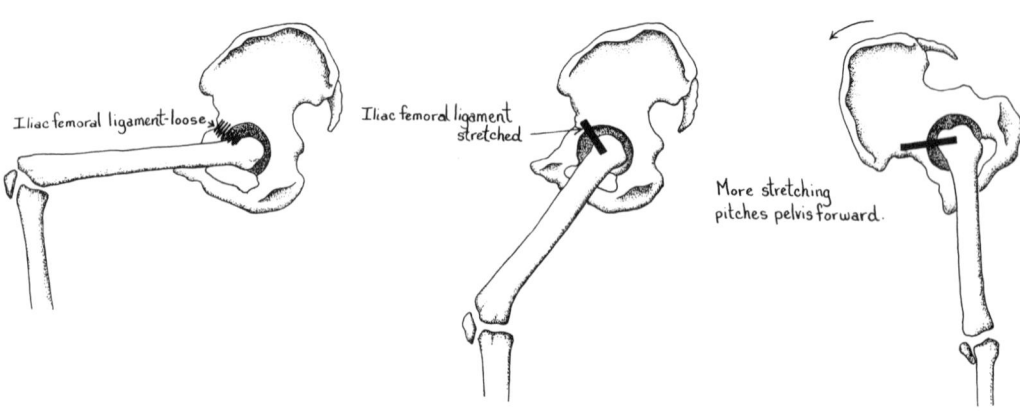

3. The degree of this problem varies from woman to woman, and those with a rather slim, male-like anatomy obviously have a definite advantage over those more feminine-looking individuals when it comes to the "standard" dressage seat.

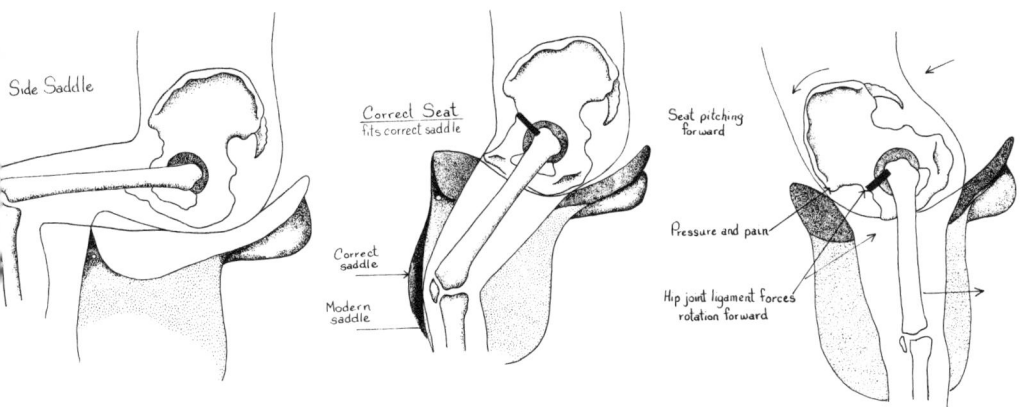

Interestingly, this issue was clearly addressed by Reiner Klimke in a clinic many years ago where he corrected lady riders who were using the long, straight-down legs which resulted in reaching down with the toes, heels up, calf, knee and thigh out of place, and an ineffective seat pitched onto the crotch, leading to overactive hands of the rider, compensating with hand riding for an ineffective seat and ineffective legs. If you look at old photographs of riders in the Olympics before 1946, or of the Spanish Riding School, you will not find those long legs as advocated by many instructors today, though without any reasonable explanation of what this is supposed to accomplish for the rider.

Therefore, recommending to lady riders that they tuck their seat under and straighten out the lordosis, while at the same time stretching their legs down or even back, makes no sense anatomically and is, for most women, an impossibility. In lor-

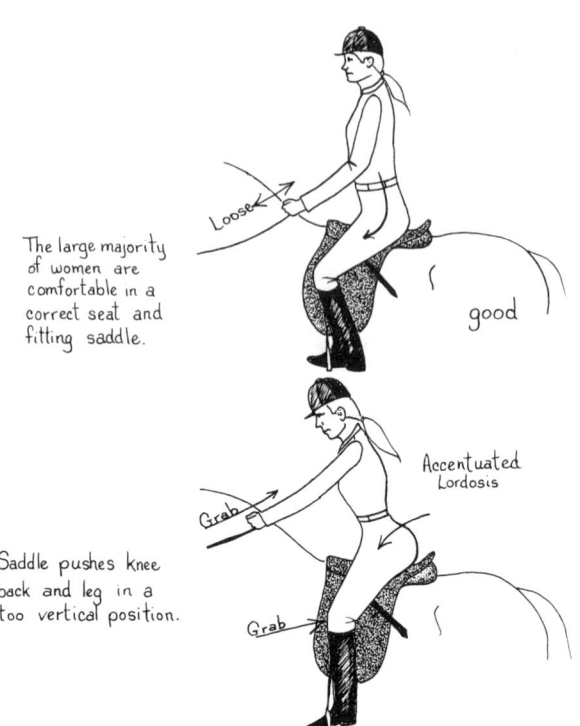

dosis, the lower lumbar spine is fixed with no lateral or longitudinal give. Further, due to its rigidity, it is prone to injuries.

From what has been said so far, it becomes evident that the kinetics of horses and humans do not match very well, and that the adjustment to the pair's harmony must be made by the human component of the team. Furthermore, the connection to the horse is the seat of the rider, which is not built to absorb motion or movements. What further complicates this situation is the fact that the basic structure of the male and female pelvises are not identical and encompass a large variation within a given range. And, historically speaking, all recommendations for an effective seat were made by men for men and often for very uniform human material, such as for the cavalry or the Spanish Riding School.

Human Biomechanics and the Seat

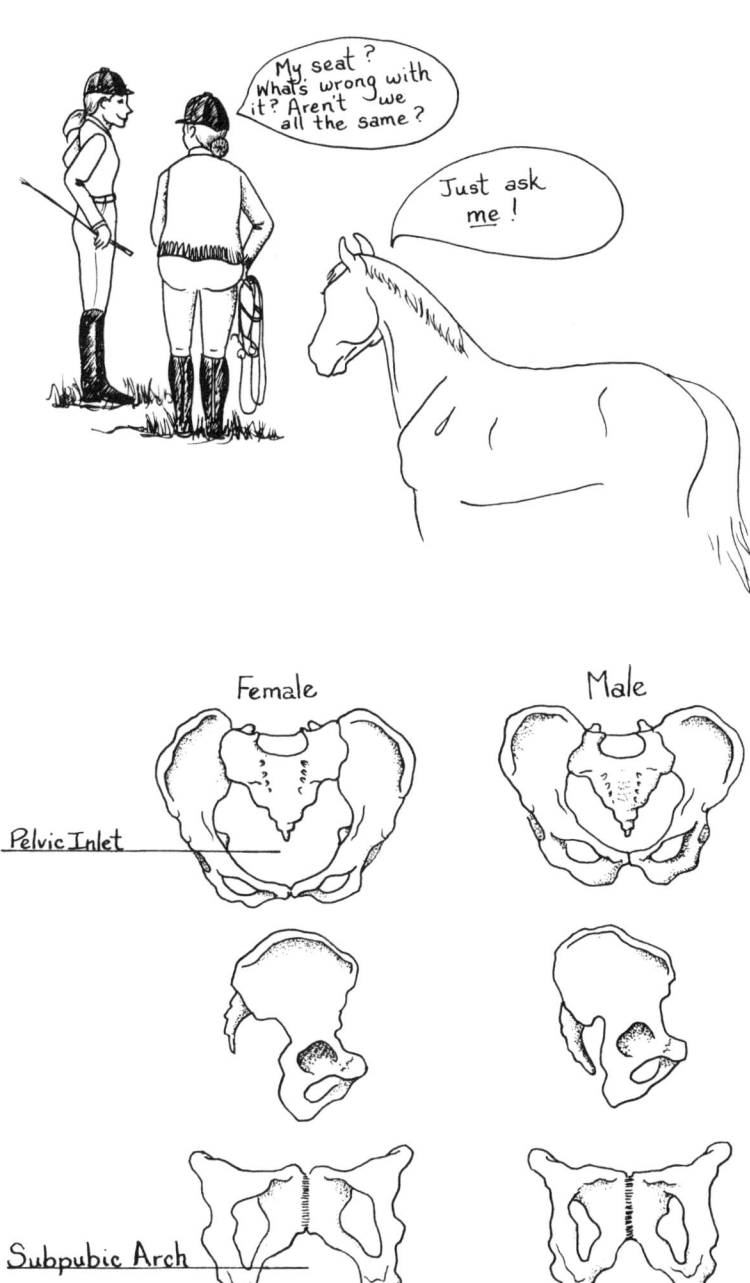

But since riding, and particularly dressage, has become an almost exclusively female sport where everybody, irrespective of body build participates, reexamining those concepts may be essential for our time. Understanding these basics is the key to it, and I hope that these short comments stimulate more discussions and thinking along those lines.

CHAPTER 7

THE LOWER SPINE

When we say that the seat must be in harmony with the movement of the horse's back, up and down, forward and backward, one side up, one side down, tilting and rotating, all simultaneously, it is clear that the pelvis, a rigid and unarticulated structure, cannot do it. So the question is, where does this very subtle but so-important adjustment originate, that ultimately leads to an established seat as we discussed earlier and called *feel*? It originates in the lower back, which must be supple and loose to compensate for the constantly changing position of the pelvis. Bracing the back will prevent this from happening. These adjustments are also totally different from the normal functions of our back.

To avoid this effort, many riders put excessive pads, rubber cushions and pillows under the saddle, absorbing all the movements of the horse's back, so they may just be sitting on top of the horse. In reality, these riders will never develop a seat or the feel and timing necessary for correct aids, as good riding requires.

When we ride, the total impact of the horse's motion and gaits is on the rider's pelvis and transmitted to the spine whether we like it or not (the exception is when we ride hunter seat in a two-point position). The objective, therefore, in teaching dressage riding is "damage control," in using the best possible position. This position ideally should allow for minimal movements of the lower spine so as to absorb as much of the motion as possible. Otherwise, there is not doubt that riding can ultimately lead to an injury of the spine and particularly to the intervertebrae disks.

The options we have are limited as follows:

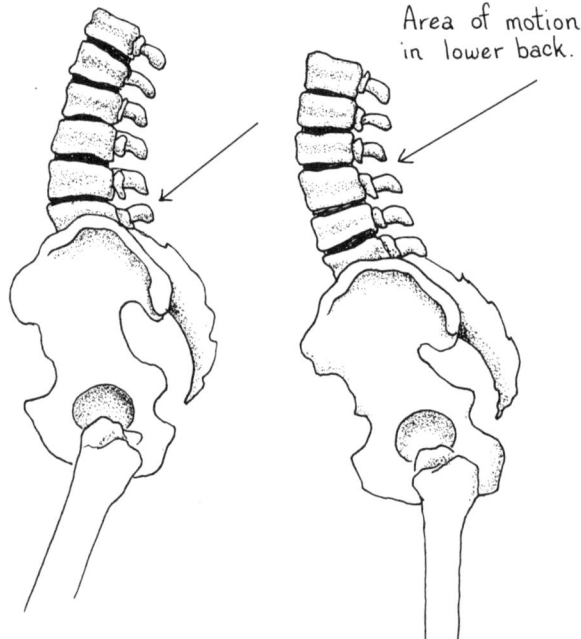

1. The mobility of the lower back, in conjunction with the abdominal muscles, can make the hip rise and fall to a certain degree on both sides, or only on one side, as well as allow for some rotation.

The Lower Spine

2. The spine itself can absorb some action by decreasing and increasing its curvature, within limits.

Looking at the construction of the spinal column, it becomes immediately evident that the intervertebral disks are the only parts that allow some mobility. The vertebrae themselves are solid, bony structures that cannot participate in this function. To accommodate the necessary movement, the arrangement of the disks should be in as neutral a position as possible. This is normally a relatively straight spine that allows bending to absorb shock combined with some lateral flexion and rotation. An excessive bend (lordosis), or fixing of the lower back, will eliminate this ability as a maximum bend is already established, and there is no elasticity or additional accommodation left. As to the muscles involved in doing so, it is particularly the abdominal muscles and not the back muscles that perform the adjustment to motion.

Therefore, we do not have only one correct seat, but each woman must sit according to her conformation or figure. Standardizing the seat in teaching is a big mistake and a sure recipe for the failure of coordination and effective aids. It can ultimately even lead to back injuries in many individuals.

The movements from an intermediate position must be learned initially by just following the movement of the horse's back. Once this has become an established reflex, based on incoming sensory impulses coming from the seat and the legs, leading to an instant adjustment and use of the abdominal muscles to adjust the position of the pelvis, the rider can proceed to deliberately using the seat to modify these responses. They then become aids either by delaying, anticipating or accentuating the reflex responses. In doing so, we are changing from passively absorbing the motion of the horse with the pelvis to actually influencing the motion to some extent. However, this is always within the natural kinetics of the horse.

We actually cannot push one side of the pelvis down since muscles only contract, but we can raise one side up by contracting the corresponding abdominal muscles, either left or right, which results automatically in the lowering of the hip on the other side. So, in riding—anatomically speaking—we adjust to the upcoming side of the horse in order to not be thrown out of the saddle. At the same time, with a relaxed back, we allow the lowering of the other side, plus a slight rotation forward.

This movement of rising on the outside and lowering of the inside, with a slight rotation forward, also affects to some

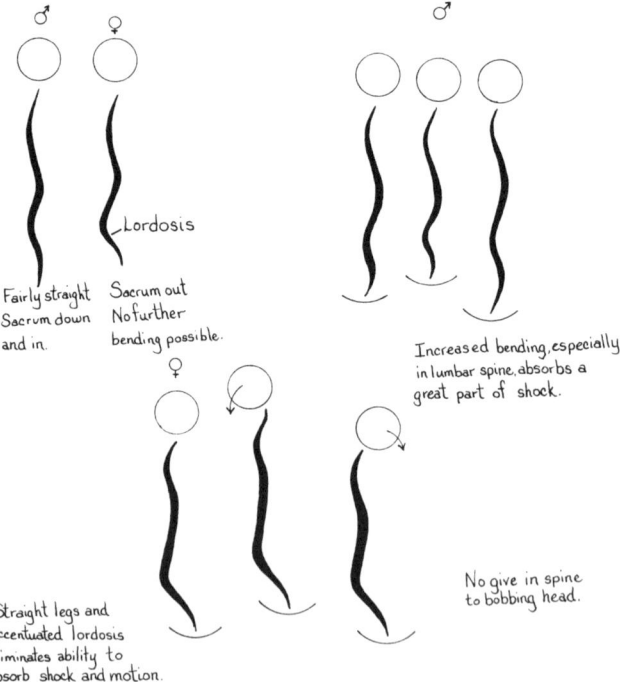

extent the position of our inside leg. The movement puts the leg of the lowered hip automatically on the horse when the horse's inside leg gets off the ground and is swinging forward, which is exactly the time when it can be influenced. When we cannot follow the movement of the horse with our pelvis, our legs become disorganized, not in rhythm with the horse's movement, and simply ineffective. Our actions, instead of being aids, become interferences.

Furthermore, a certain misalignment of hips and shoulders, leading to unequal leg position, further aggravates the already disorganized aids. And we are all rather one-sided, mostly right-handed, with a more or less pronounced scoliosis. In the beginning, when we are first learning to ride, this position prevents us from sitting symmetrically. The incorrect alignment of the shoulders and the hips leads to an unbalanced seat, an unequal leg position, unequal movements, and a crooked position with a collapsed hip, often accentuated by stirrups of unequal length.

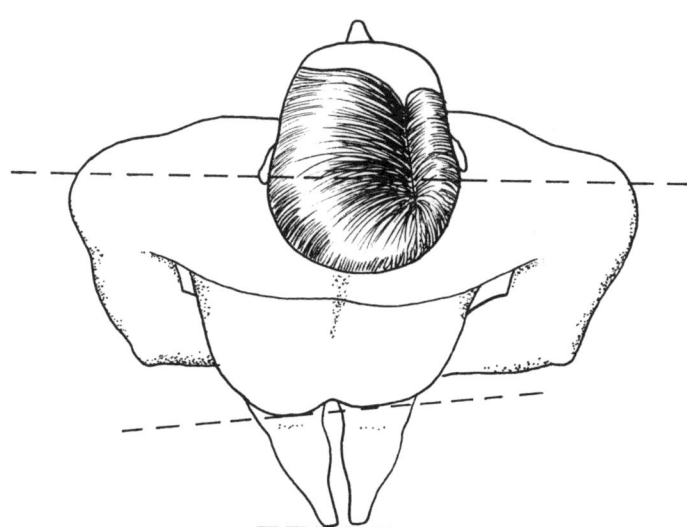

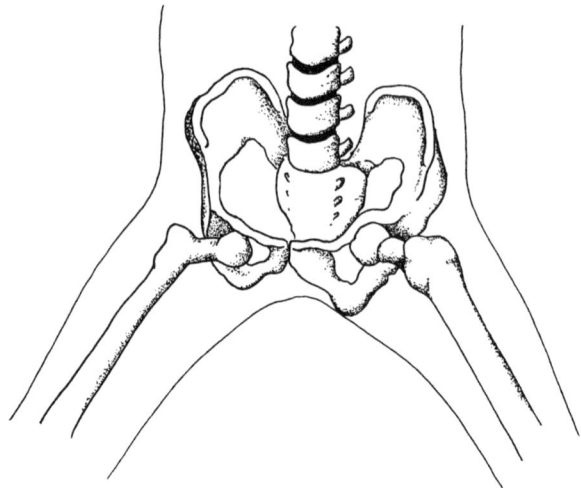

In teaching, advising the rider to keep his or her hands steady, or to "follow the motion of the horse," is perfectly useless since the hand's movements depend on the steadiness of

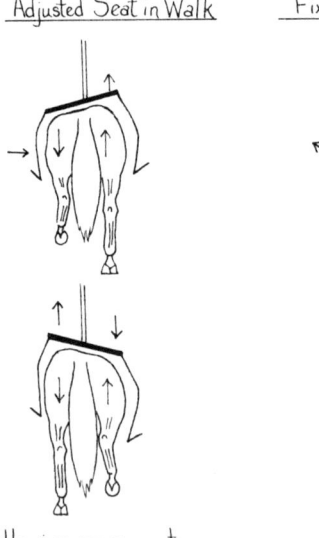
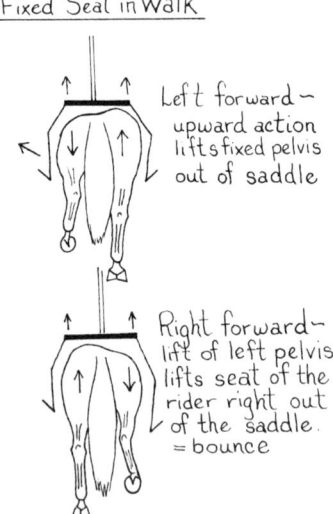

Following movement of back – same mechanism takes place but faster and stronger in the sitting trot.

THE LOWER SPINE

Walk
with human kinetics

Left hindleg forward.
Horse's hip sinks down. Belly swings to right.
Rider's left hand relaxes.

Left front leg forward
Left horse's hip back up, side strides forward
Rider's hip follows forward but shoulder and
arm move back.

the upper body. And that can only be achieved with a correct seat. So we come back to the old saying that there are no good hands without a good seat.

Yes, good hands are only possible from a confirmed seat. But this is even more true for the legs which are directly attached to the pelvic structure. Until a confirmed seat has been achieved, no correct or timed leg aids are possible. A beginner rider is in perfect harmony at the rising trot, with the rhythm of one of the horse's hind legs, depending on the diagonal he is using. But in the sitting trot, this coordination disappears, the legs are banging on the horse's sides; they're not controlled or in rhythm with the horse. The problem here is not the legs, but the not-yet-established seat.

Looked at from this perspective, the training program of the Spanish Riding School makes eminent sense. Student riders there concentrate for the first two years on being lunged with-

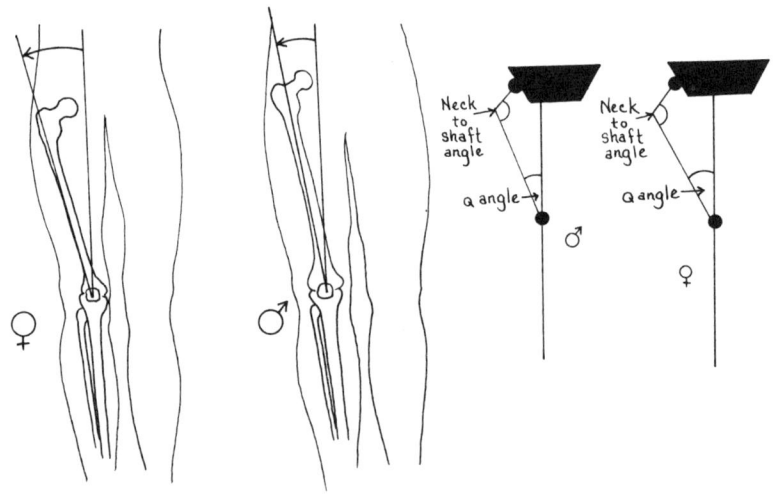

Effect of width of pelvis on position on femur and its ability to spread out over back of horse.

out stirrups or reins, until a confirmed, independent seat is achieved. Only then are the students allowed to use stirrups and, later, reins, but only under close supervision of their instructors.

Considering all the problems we face as riders, maybe we should establish a training pyramid for riders so they can become capable of implementing the training pyramid for horses, a scale that has proven its value over and over again. Wouldn't this be a terrific subject for another book....?

CHAPTER 8

THE SEAT AND THE SADDLE

For thousands of years, riders sat on their horses without saddles or stirrups, leading to a much better coordination and harmony of their kinetics. However, with the introduction of saddles by the Romans and Chinese, a new element was interjected between horse and rider. The argument about what is right or wrong about this has been with us ever since. This varies depending on what was or is expected between horse and rider, which is obviously different between, say, riding in a jousting tournament in the Middle Ages and a modern-day dressage test. The following comments and illustrations relate only to one aspect, that is, the anatomy and kinetics of riders in relation to our present day aspirations and the saddles we use.

Those anatomical considerations we discussed in the previous chapter should not only be applied to how we sit when riding, but to the construction and shape of the saddle. While it is generally common knowledge that a saddle must fit the horse's back, withers and general conformation, very little has been done to build the saddle in accordance with the anatomy and conformation of the female rider.

If you look at historical photographs,* you might notice that up until 1980, dressage saddles were built forward, to accommodate the correct position of the thigh and to keep the rider's knee within the knee roll of the saddle. There is no comparison in comfort from these older saddles to the present straight, unisex saddles. I can personally attest to this since my wife's and my own hunt and dressage saddles were made by the same saddle maker according to our own different conformations and builds.

Let's look at the same saddle in relation to a male and female pelvis.

THE FEMALE

The female's broader pelvic arch often leads to impact on the soft tissue of the crotch. The more the rider stretch her legs down, the worse off she is as she is pitched forward, and the more pressure on the soft tissue, without being compensated by a bony structure.

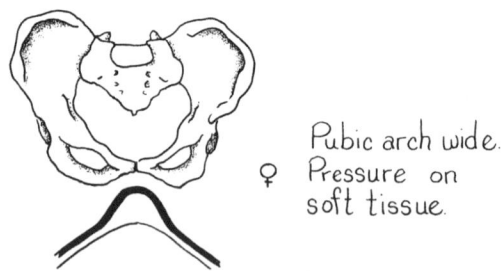

---

* I recommend spending some time with two books in particular: **Klimke on Dressage** by Reiner Klimke, published by my publisher Half Halt Press, Inc. and **Das Dressur Pferd** by Harry Boldt, published by Editions Haberbeck in 1978. By carefully studying the photographs, you will learn a great deal about the issues discussed in this chapter—plus, it is a fascinating exercise.

THE MALE

The male's narrow pelvic arch makes contact with the saddle, avoiding pressure on the soft tissue. The male rider can stretch his legs down without changing the contact.

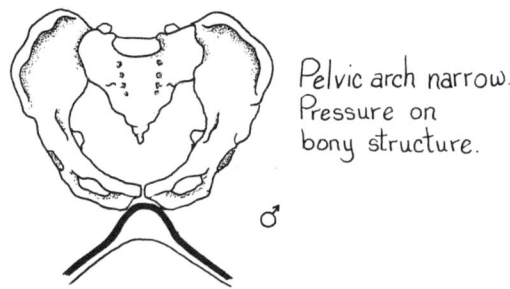

Pelvic arch narrow. Pressure on bony structure.

Today, most dressage saddles go straight down, vertically from the pommel. They are often promoted and attached to the name of a present-day famous rider who would very often not even dream of sitting in the saddle himself.

These vertically built saddles with the hefty knee rolls have two basic unfavorable effects on the seat and can only be used by very, very few riders. These two effects are:

1. If the knee is kept truly in the correct position within the knee roll, the thigh is then pushed too far back, pitching a woman onto her crotch and producing a very accentuated lordosis.

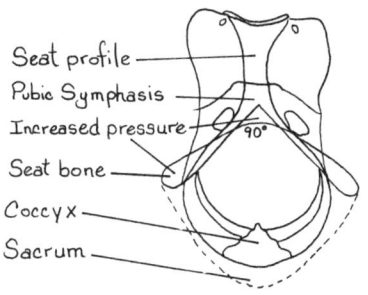

The more the lordosis is accentuated, the more pressure is put on the most forward support point, the pubic area, and the crotch.

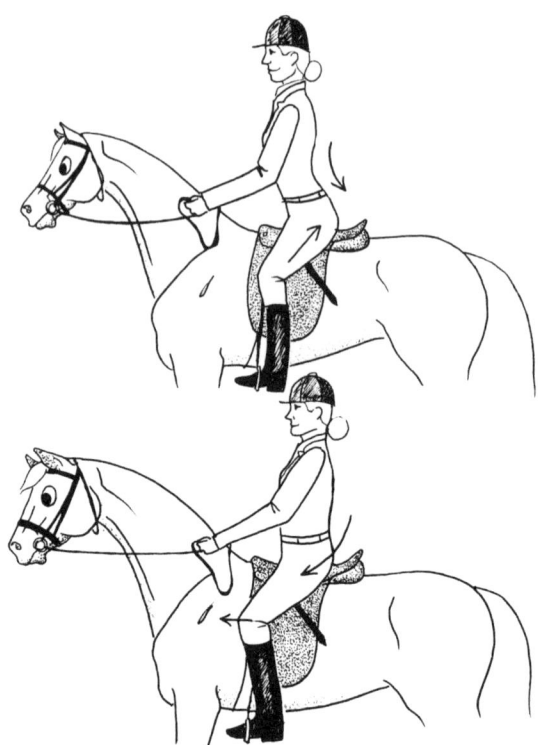

2. What we see most frequently, however, is that the rider's knee is pushed over and ahead of the saddle and the knee roll, forcing the thigh to rotate out, the spurs to rotate in—basically unseating the rider!

Maybe the time has come for saddle makers to rethink the concept and truly build saddles that not only accommodate the pelvic conformation of their customer, but also the anatomical limitations in the position of his or her thighs.

Based on the female's anatomy of the pelvis, saddle makers should experiment with the following designs (and lady riders buying a new saddle should also keep these considerations in mind).

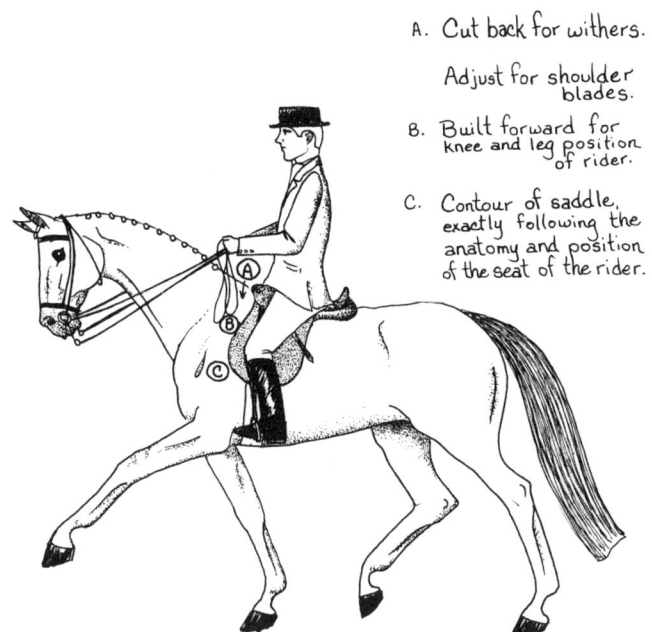

A. Cut back for withers. Adjust for shoulder blades.

B. Built forward for knee and leg position of rider.

C. Contour of saddle, exactly following the anatomy and position of the seat of the rider.

1. The wider female pelvis should get better support from a wider seat.

2. The design should be flatter for women than it is for men.

3. The pommel should be wider, allowing for the pubic arch to rest on the saddle, and not on the soft part of the crotch.

4. Saddle flaps should be built more forward, and knee rolls not so exaggerated which only pushes the rider's thighs outward, leading to an incorrect leg position.

5. The women's saddle should accommodate a more flexed leg position than for men.

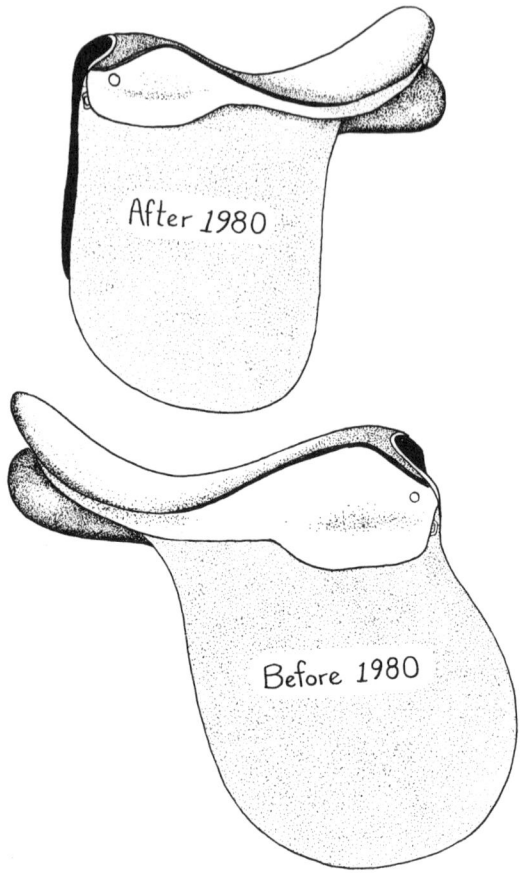

Taking the concept of a well-fitting saddle a step further, it is just as important that it follows and fits the rider as well as the horse. Even the best saddle for the horse, if it does not conform to the body build of the rider, is the origin of lots of problems and difficulties which are then blamed on the horse.

In addition, saddles which have practically no pads fit the horse and rider better, and allow for a much better interaction of horse and rider.

Here is Josef Neckermann riding two different horses in two Olympics. In the top photo, he is riding in his old saddle which fits him like a glove. In the lower photo he is riding in a modern saddle and his knee is over the flap and his heels up.

Henry Chammartin, Swiss Cavalry, won on a saddle made by Niefenegger in Bern especially for this horse and rider.

This is as close to perfection as you will ever see. The seat and legs of the rider look perfectly quiet in the medium to extended trot. Now look at the following charachteristics of the saddle:

1. A slight cut back at the withers to allow for the freedom of the shoulder blade, and as a consequence the reach of the front legs.

2. The front of the saddle is exactly molded to the leg position of the rider from top to bottom.

3. The thigh and the knee are inside the knee roll.

4. The side flaps are long enough to accomodate the then fashionable slightly shorter boots of the rider.

5. The saddle pad is a soft leather over a very thin layer of felt, transmitting all the movements of the horse through the saddle to the rider.

What a difference!

These two photos show a junior rider, relaxed in an all-purpose saddle that fits her anatomy and conformation. The saddle also fits her horse who is moving forward nicely and looking very happy and relaxed. Just look at the size of stride this rider gets from her mount in the top photo.

But then comes the dressage lesson in the lower photo: the stirrups have come down two or three holes, the leg position is ruined, she now sits on her crotch, way back on the saddle with no support for her legs which are now turned out. The forward gait of her horse is gone. These are two really unhappy campers. Now the question worth asking is: is this position really the basis of dressage?

CHAPTER 9

THE THREE GAITS OF HUMAN AND HORSE

After considering in the preceding chapters various aspects of the biomechanics of the horse and rider, and each's kinetics in relation to movement and balance, I'd like make some comments on the gaits. These might seem to relate primarily to the beginner rider, but I hope they serve as a review and reminder to no-longer-beginners. These comments point to some areas that are essential to making progress in dressage. The understanding of what needs to be done will not shorten the time to develop the correct reflexes or better control over the body, but will at least prevent useless and counterproductive attempts to be repeated over and over again without success, but developed instead into bad habits and reflexes.

We are often told that we will know it when we have developed feel, but how is "feel" really defined? I think feel is defined by these two things: first, by following the movements of horse using the input of the seat in your reflex system. Secondly, it is automatically anticipating the effects of the centers of mass and gravity as needed (remember, the effects of these centers are continuously changing). In all three gaits, our kinetics must adjust to the horse to get the best kinetics from him, and when this has developed to the point of being automatic, we can be said to have "feel."

To develop a seat that properly integrates into the movement of the horse's back in all three gaits, keep in mind the following concepts.

The movement of the horse's back has two phases, one upward and forward from the impulsion of the hind legs, leading to suspension followed by a downward motion due to gravity, which is stopped by the impact of the front legs when touching the ground. This repeats itself over and over for every stride. The other phase is as one side of the back reaches down and forward, alternating from side to side, and at every stride as the front legs touch the ground. Then, a sort of braking action takes place as the front legs touch the ground. Once the front legs become vertical, the pushing action of the hind legs creates impulsion. The center of mass opposes this happening and, if not compensated for by the rider, it leads to dropping back and forth consistently against the horse's motion.

Therefore, the movements of the horse's back are strictly conditioned by the footfall of the legs on their impact transmitted when touching down and on the impulsion upward and forward when pushing off.

This varies from gait to gait, and our seat must adapt to it.

In this section, I will not discuss the aids in riding as there are innumerable good books on the market as well as magazines dealing with their use on a continuous basis.

It does not matter which riding approach or theory and training methods you follow, but the process of developing horse related kinetics and reflexes remains the same irrespective of the method you adopt. And, irrespective of what method you decide upon, gravity, center of mass and their affect will be with you at every stride from the time you mount your horse.

THE WALK

The walk is considered the most difficult gait and the one most easily ruined. All the imperfections in training and riding show up very early in the walk and are the ones most difficult to correct. Here again is the quote from the FEI and AHSA *Rule Books*:

It is at the pace of walk that the imperfections of dressage are most evident. This is also the reason why a horse should not be asked to walk on the bit at the early stages of training. A too precipitated collection will not only spoil the collected walk but the medium and extended walk as well.

To this statement, many others add that the quality of the walk also affects negatively the quality of the canter.

Despite the difficulty in maintaining correctness in the walk, for the beginner rider the walk is the most comfortable and secure of the three gaits. Since the beginner rider has absolutely no perception of what the horse is doing to keep moving in balance, he or she is perfectly happy to be sitting there and rocking back and forth. He has no idea that the horse has to move its center of gravity into a new triangle of support at every stride, as explained in the first chapter of this book, and since he does not interfere with it, everything is fine.

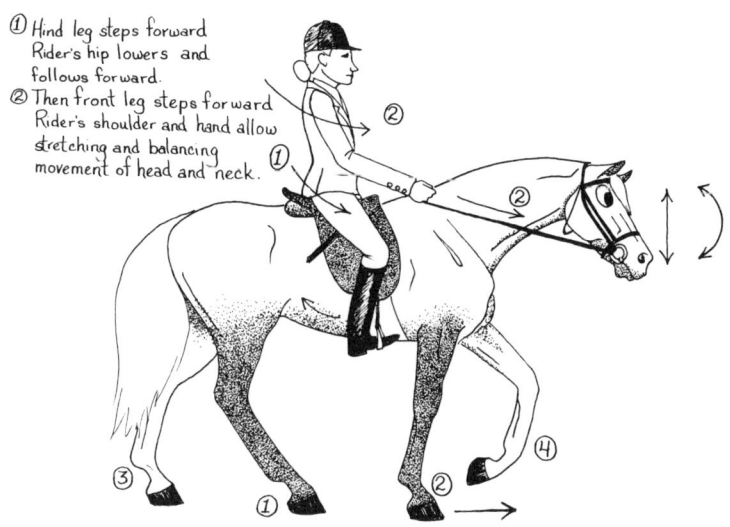

Correct aids for walk

Problems begin to come when the rider tries to organize the walk to his or her concepts before being aware of what is happening under him. An old adage is that you should not try to teach a horse collection in the walk before you can teach—not just ride—a collected trot and canter. This is the basis of why the collected walk is only asked for in Fourth Level tests and, even then, only to what is feasible and reasonable for a given horse and its conformation.

A restriction in front and a vertical head carriage have nothing to do with collection. Instead, collection must come from behind, not from the front, and must remain active. Often, an incorrect approach leads to a lateral walk or the pacing seen, unfortunately, in so many upper level horses. Most of those riders do not truly understand the walk and have no idea of how to go about fixing it. Unfortunately, many wonderful young horses are ruined by ignorance and the lack of knowledge.

Unless you have a full understanding and feeling of the kinetics of the horse walking under you, based on keeping the

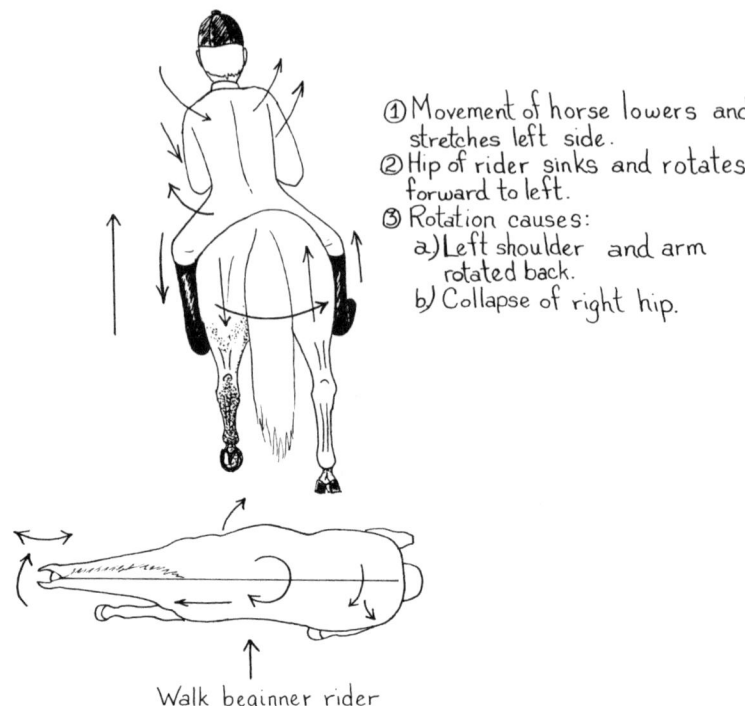

Walk beginner rider

correct balance, you should not try to interfere with the walk. Once you do begin to work on the walk, it must be within the correct arrangement of the movement and the footfalls of the horse, and not against it. This is the basis of the FEI and AHSA *Rule Book* statements.

Looking at the illustrations, you will note that we must have an independence, soft seat in the rhythm of the hind legs coming off the ground and reaching forward. We allow with our fingers a slight opening of the rein just as the front leg on the same side is leaving the ground. This must happen sequentially and not simultaneously, as the walk is a four-beat gait.

The Three Gaits of Human and Horse 117

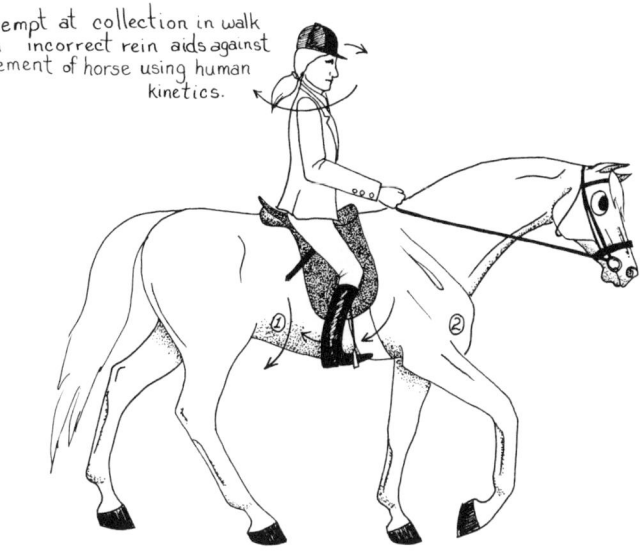

Walk: aids against horse = → pacing

As for collection, it must be ridden from your seat and legs in harmony with the movement of the haunches, and not from the hands, restricting balance and footfall in front.

The Trot

The trot is by far the steadiest and best balanced gait for the horse. For this reason, it is the gait generally used in the training of the horse by accomplished riders. But for the beginner, the trot is a real problem because of the sitting trot. The inability to sit to the trot by the beginner rider, causing a relentless pounding on the back, resulted in the decision of those responsible for the 1995 and 1999 tests to allow rising trot at the discretion of the rider in both Training Level 1 and 2. The test designers were trying to take pity on the poor horses who are consistently abused by the inability of their riders. Banging legs and bouncing seats really have nothing to do with dressage which is based on the harmony of horse and rider; this should be the very first objective.

The reason for this bouncy sitting trot is the lack of the following seat of the rider. And this lack is caused very often by excessively stretching down and trying to have a long leg, which puts the seat on the crotch and results in a fixed lordosis. The rider then tries to support his balance by hanging onto the reins (imagine the poor horse's mouth!) and clamping on with his legs. No wonder horses hollow their backs and come off the bit in the sitting trot! So very often we see just that, but as soon as the rider moves into a rising trot or even a canter (which has even easier kinetics to follow), the horse begins rounding his back and coming back onto the bit. This hollowing of the back and coming up with the head in the sitting trot is not a misbehaving by the horse, but simply his last defense against an injurious rider.

The basic problem here, as we know by now, is the rider's seat (or lack of!). And the development of the seat takes time since nobody's pelvis was ever intended to walk, trot and canter and follow the movement of a horse's back. Very often, just shortening the stirrups to suit the rider's body build and not insisting on a fixed, preconceived idea of long legs is very helpful.

While the horse has only one trot, the kinetics of which were explained in the first chapter, we have developed three approaches to riding it: the rising trot, the sitting trot and the two-point position. Since the trot is the best balanced gait for carrying weight, with the center of gravity always supported by one diagonal, it is the preferred gait for the basic training of the horse. This is reflected in the lower level dressage tests which have more trot movements. When we ask for new movements, we always ask for them first in the trot or walk and only when the horses have understood it, in the canter. This includes movements such as collection, lateral work, half pass and pirouettes.

In the trot, the movements of the horse's back are dictated by the transmission of energy from the haunches forward. This causes the back to round upward at every stride, and is further enhanced by the suspension which gets progressively more powerful as we move to medium and extended trot. In addition, there is a lateral movement from left to right and a stretching forward when the front legs reach out.

As noted previously, the more suspension, fluidity and cadence, the more difficult it is to sit the trot. This is further complicated in the extended trot where, in addition to the above-mentioned back movement, it becomes even more difficult to cope with impulsion, velocity and the opposing factor of the center of mass. It is not surprising that the sitting trot is by far the most difficult of the gaits to conquer. But it is also the most essential to learn properly since the ability to sit this gait is a dressage basic from Second Level on.

The importance of this was perhaps best stated by Nuno Oliveira:

The rider who is not properly in the saddle, supple, as one with the horse can never achieve any independence between the various aids, a condition sine qua non to insure good hands and leg aids.

2 Point Position

Shorter stirrups.
Center of gravity over feet.
Motion of horse absorbed by legs.
Center of mass controlled by upper body and legs.
= Human Balance Mechanisms.

THE TWO-POINT POSITION

Trotting along in a two-point position is the surest approach to avoid the difficulties we've been discussing as the entire motion of the horse can be absorbed by the same mechanism we humans use when standing on our feet. And when you rest your hands on the horse's neck, you have one more support point to help keep your balance.

At the same time, though, by removing your pelvis from the motion of the horse's back, you also eliminate any possibility to influence the horse from your seat. You are nothing else but a passenger. While this is a common position in jumping, cross-country riding and hunting, it is not done in dressage for this reason.

THE RISING TROT

On the other hand, the rising trot is the most ingenious solution to integrate the separate kinetics of horse and rider. It uses the velocity of the horse's back movement with gravity's effect on the rider in such a way as to make the rising trot almost effortless and very comfortable for horse and rider. Certainly, the beginning rider strains and does the movement artificially as we can see in any riding school, but he or she soon learns to let it happen with less and less effort.

Because we post on one diagonal of the trot only, the position of the horse's back is always the same for that fraction of the second when we are in the saddle. This avoids the problem for the humans of having to force the pelvis to follow the motion of the horse's back.

In addition, at the rising trot we do not have to compensate with our spine for the up and down of the horse's back as we allow the velocity of the upward motion to go unchecked and lift us out of the saddle. Then, without us having to do anything about it, gravity brings us back down into the saddle for a fraction of a second, just to start the sequence all over again.

By just letting this happen, it can be the easiest way to learn about timing and rhythm, and how far we get out of the saddle depends entirely on the horse.

The beginner as well as the advanced rider feels comfortable with this approach as it combines the natural shock absorption of our legs (which is hardly needed) and avoids the necessity of a steady, following seat as in the sitting trot to compensate for gravity and velocity. This also avoids putting any excessive demands on the horse's back.

Since this is a one-sided approach as far as the muscular effort of the horse is concerned, it has been recommended to change the diagonal regularly. However, since horses are not symmetrical or ambidextrous, they always prefer one side or the other and have an uncanny ability to put the rider on the diagonal they prefer. You feel a difference in comfort on a young horse if you post left or right, something that will disappear with progressive training, straightness and the development of equal pushing and supporting power of the haunches, but it will always remain a minimal factor.

This has been known to the cavalry for years, and the instruction to change diagonals is in all cavalry manuals. This is probably best documented in the recommendation to the participants of the endurance ride from Berlin to Vienna without a break, a stretch of 620 km, that took place in the late 1800s. For the first half or two-thirds of the distance, the rec-

Rising trot in sitting phase.
Rider's inside leg on horse when inside hind leg of horse leaves the ground.

Rising trot out of saddle, right diagonal

ommendation was that riders should scrupulously change diagonals regularly. But when the horse began to tire, the rider should allow the horse to select the diagonal that the horse felt more comfortable in. The best time for covering this distance was 72 hours in uninterrupted progression.

We have all been admonished to ride the horse from "your inside leg to your outside rein," by using your inside calf at the same time the inside hind leg moves off the ground and, if needed, closing the fingers of your outside hand to steady the rhythm. We know that the only hind leg that can respond to your leg is the one that does not carry any weight. Therefore, the effectiveness of your aids is not force, but timing, which becomes absolutely automatic in the rising trot, depending on which side you select.

In the rising trot, whenever we sit down our legs come on the horse's flank and mainly on the inside. This causes a mus-

cular contraction, pulling the leg forward and inward exactly at the time when the inside hind leg of the horse gets off the ground and swings forward. And since the horse dictates the rhythm of our rising trot, the timing is always perfect.

Back in the 50s, I was riding at Sunnyfield Farm with one of the great European masters who was teaching our team. I asked him the question about which diagonal was correct for the rising trot and the answer was very simple: there is no right or wrong diagonal, it simply depends on which hind leg you want to influence.

This is what the AHSA *Rule Book* basically refers to: All trot to be done sitting unless otherwise specified. But when you look at the lower level dressage tests where rising trot is asked for or allowed, it never says left or right diagonal, giving the educated rider a choice to present the horse at its best.

THE SITTING TROT

The sitting trot is, without any doubt, the most difficult movement to learn as the pelvic and sacroiliac structure of the rider must adjust to the motion of the horse's back, and develop reflexes originating from the seat, leading to a completely new pattern of kinetics. If not accomplished, the proper coordination and action of the rider's legs and hands are impossible, as is the ability to use the weight aids without moving the seat (or for that matter, the upper body), often leading to a collapsed hip.

We even see riders in the upper levels having difficulty in riding the sitting trot, where the continuous banging of the legs and unsteady hands clearly indicates that they have not yet achieved it. The key to failure or success in dressage is the ability to correctly sit the trot and it is very important to be able to understand the complexity of this task.

This quote from Hans von Heydelbrek, writing in 1929 in **Die Deutsche Dressur Preufung** says it all:

The sophistication of the rider is clearly demonstrated by his seat and his influence and effectiveness (weight aids). The quieter and more effective these aids are, the higher the equestrian skill of the riders. Not the stiff upper body position but the soft incorporation into the motion of the horse is the hallmark of a good seat. In judging a dressage test, the seat of the rider becomes a determining factor.

Now from the horse's point of view, the trot is the same if you are in a two-point position, a rising trot or a sitting trot. But in the first two we either completely avoid the kinetics of the horse or allow their influence to our advantage by establishing harmony between horse and rider while still relying on

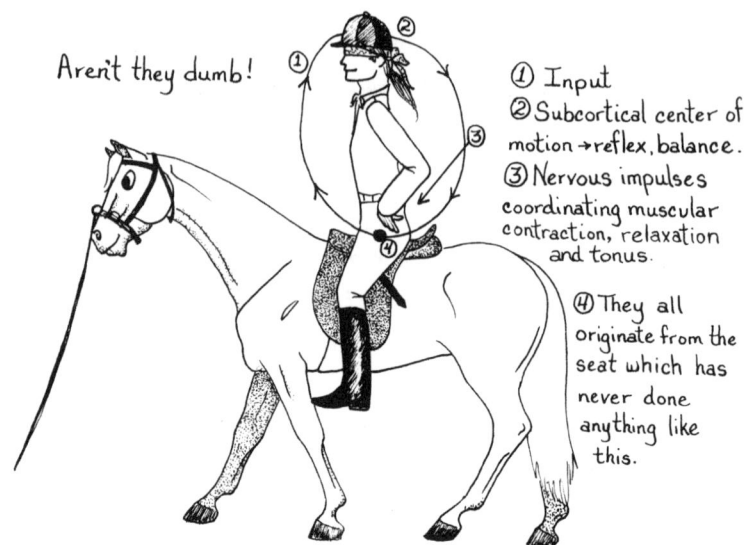

our human reflexes for balance. This simply does not work anymore when riding the sitting trot.

A horse with a big trot with lots of cadence and suspension is a recipe of failure for the beginner, whereas an old school horse just plodding along is much better and less frustrating. So what is the problem? It is that while sitting the trot, our pelvis is in contact with a base that rises and falls, and pivots from one side to the other, and reaches forward on the side it lowers, into the leading front leg. This is more than our seat can handle initially, and the normal human reaction is to clamp with the legs and fix the pelvis position, which is exactly the opposite of what should happen.

The lungeing of a beginner in the trot for almost two years without stirrups and reins as done in the Spanish Riding School simply establishes a new reflex system, the origin and the end point being the pelvis structure including the lower spine and the entire musculature apparatus connecting it. The wisdom of this technique of training is clear, but in reality who has the two years?

Many professionals who ride four to eight horses a day have a tremendous advantage over an amateur who has only one horse and often cannot even ride everyday.

If you watch a Second or Third Level dressage test, the differences often become striking. There is the rider with a confirmed seat who has quiet legs he can use at will, left or right, and in the rhythm of the hind legs of the horse. The amateur rider, even when trying to sit pretty with his upper body, has nothing but banging legs, totally out of control and not coordinated with the hind legs of the horse. No wonder these horses get dull and frustrated.

There is no doubt that in our country we do not spend enough time on the lunge line and, as a result, do not develop a correct seat, legs and hands, and often get stuck at Second or Third Level.

Considering the difficulty for adult riders to develop new reflexes for a true sitting trot, I think thought should be given to allowing adult amateur classes to have all medium and extended trots ridden in rising trot as an option. Historically speaking, this was done by the FEI and AHSA up until 1972.

THE MISCONCEPTION OF THE DRIVING SEAT

As bad and counterproductive as pulling a horse into a tight frame and behind the vertical, it is even worse to expect the horse to go forward in self-carriage when the rider leans behind the vertical, pushing the horse's back down, on the assumption that this is driving the horse forward into a medium or extended trot and canter.

Let's examine this position from the two basic factors, the center of gravity and center of mass, and see what happens.

THE CENTER OF GRAVITY

When the rider is leaning behind the vertical, the center of gravity is no longer above the base of support, which is the seat. If not compensated for, this throws the rider's upper body even farther back, and if unopposed, falling on the horse's rump. Then the compensatory mechanisms come into play:

First, the rider tries to hang on using the reins and the horse's mouth, which results in exactly the opposite of what is requested by the AHSA and FEI rules. Or, the rider clamps on the legs, which prevents him or her from using synchronized leg aids with the kinetics of the horse's gaits.

The rider has no choice but to compensate like this because no object can stay in balance when the center of gravity falls outside of its base of support.

The following quotes from the FEI and AHSA *Rule Books* are very clear and explain that this is exactly what should not be done.

MEDIUM TROT

The rider allows the horse remaining 'on the bit' to carry his head a little more in front of the vertical than at the collected or working trot, and allows him at the same time to lower his head and neck slightly.

EXTENDED TROT

The rider allows the horse remaining 'on the bit' without leaning on it to lengthen his frame and to gain ground.

MEDIUM CANTER

The rider allows the horse remaining 'on the bit' to carry his head a little more in front of the vertical than at the collected or working canter and allows him at the same time to lower his head and neck slightly.

EXTENDED CANTER

The rider allows the horse remaining 'on the bit' without leaning on it to lower and extend his neck, the tip of his nose pointing more or less forward.

The simplest and most effective way to allow the horse to move in front of the vertical is for the rider to lower the position of his hands by one or two inches and to open slightly the fingers on the reins. To regain the collection, it is sufficient to raise your hands up again, and drive with your seat against a holding hand.

Doing it this way automatically brings your upper body slightly forward, keeping the center of gravity solidly supported as well as compensated for by the effect of the center of mass against impulsion as explained in the following paragraphs.

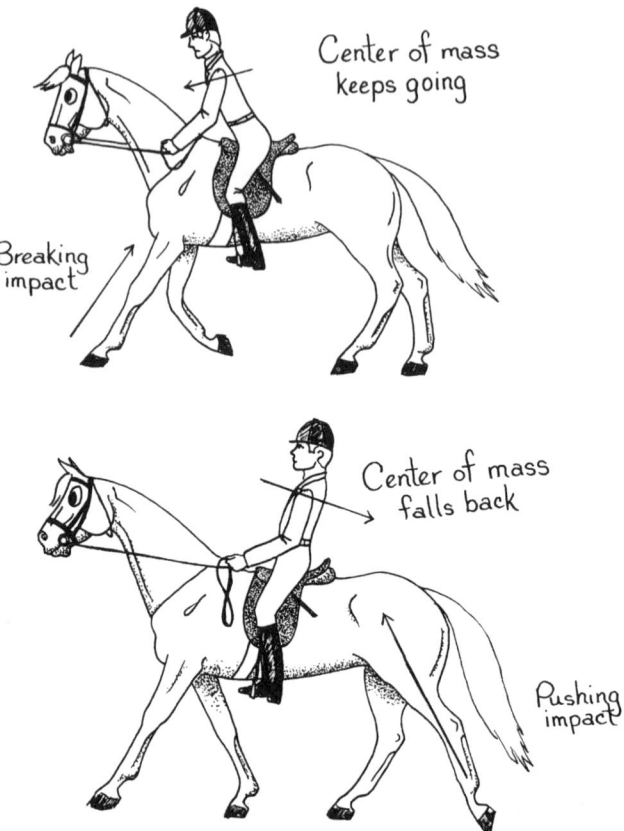

THE CENTER OF MASS

The effect of the center of mass of the rider is another and even more important factor here as it opposes the kinetics of the horse as expressed by the push and impulsion forward in the medium and extended gaits. The effect of the center of mass is to throw the rider backward and out of balance at every stride if not compensated for.

The works of Dr. Hilary Clayton are useful for understanding the alternating braking and pushing impulses emanating from all three gaits which impact on the rider's body.

The Three Gaits of Human and Horse

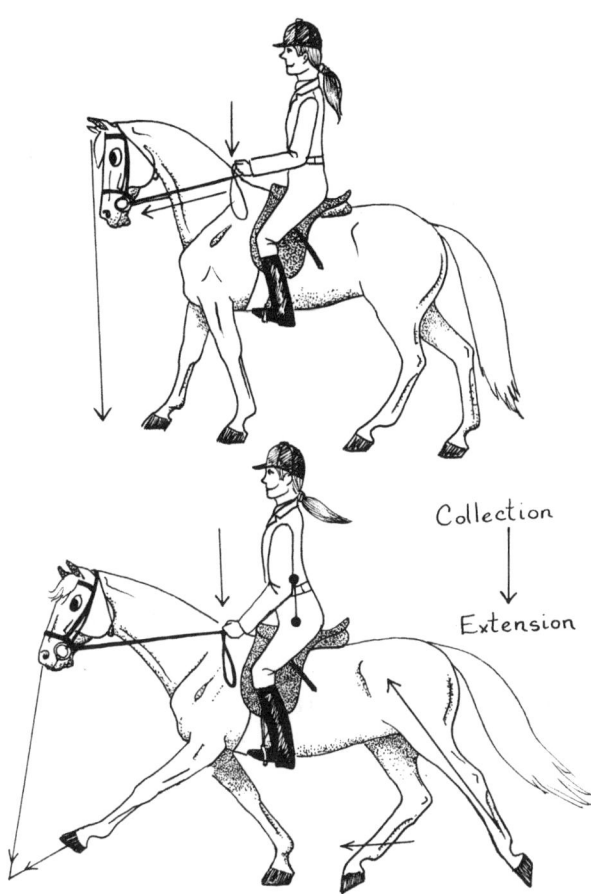

Collection ↓ Extension

Each time there is a braking movement from the horse, the rider's center of the mass throws him forward. Each time there is a push from the horse's impulsion, coming from the haunches, the rider's center of mass throws him back at every stride if not anticipated and compensated for. But with a rider already behind the motion, with his center of gravity behind the base of support, it is a disaster for the poor horse.

Nothing like this is encountered by the human body under normal circumstances, so humans are unprepared to cope with

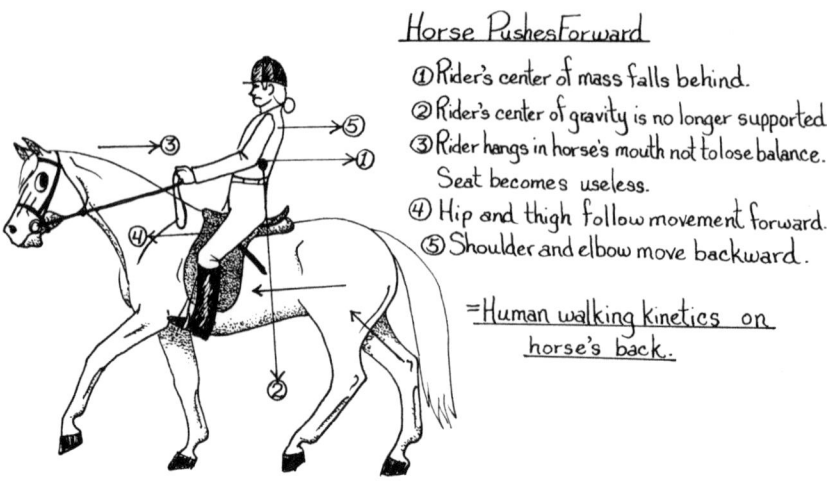

Horse Pushes Forward
① Rider's center of mass falls behind.
② Rider's center of gravity is no longer supported.
③ Rider hangs in horse's mouth not to lose balance. Seat becomes useless.
④ Hip and thigh follow movement forward.
⑤ Shoulder and elbow move backward.

= Human walking kinetics on horse's back.

Wrong canter depart

this effect when they start riding. There are no reflexes originating in the seat, going to the subcortical center and back to all the muscles that coordinate our seat and position.

Anticipating and compensating for this effect, together with this ability to use the pelvic structure and its limited ability effectively is the basis on which we develop a correct seat and later feel.

THE CANTER

There is an old truism that when a rider shows a poor or incorrect walk, the canter is usually not better and is also impaired. The reason is not the horse, but that the same human kinetics that ruin the walk similarly interfere with the canter.

The illustrations in this section show clearly what goes wrong and why we cannot move the same way on horseback as we do when we are on our own feet. Here, as with the walk, it is the rider's inside shoulder and arm that come back as the hip moves forward together with the motion of the horse. This is

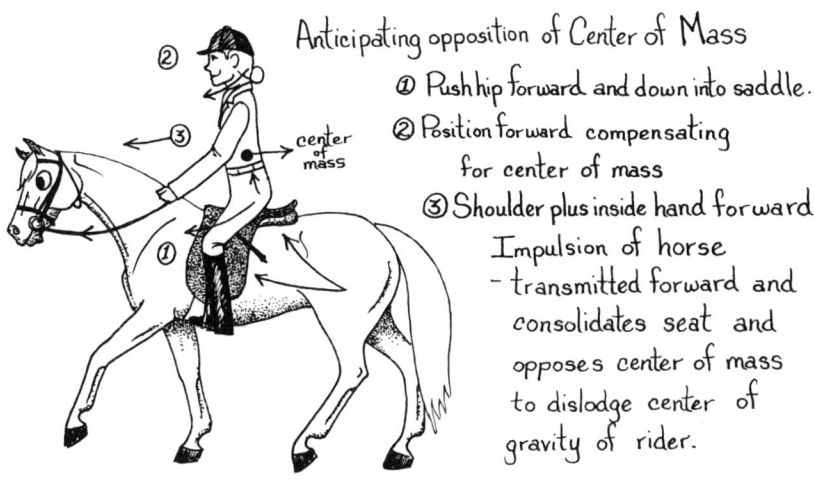

Anticipating opposition of Center of Mass
① Push hip forward and down into saddle.
② Position forward compensating for center of mass
③ Shoulder plus inside hand forward.
Impulsion of horse
- transmitted forward and consolidates seat and opposes center of mass to dislodge center of gravity of rider.

Correct canter depart

even more accentuated by the effect of the center of mass that pulls the rider backward, opposing the impulsion generated by the haunches and the forward velocity. Not only does the inside shoulder and arm come back, an insecure rider must balance himself with anything he can hold onto, and by consequence, steadies himself on the horse's mouth by clutching the

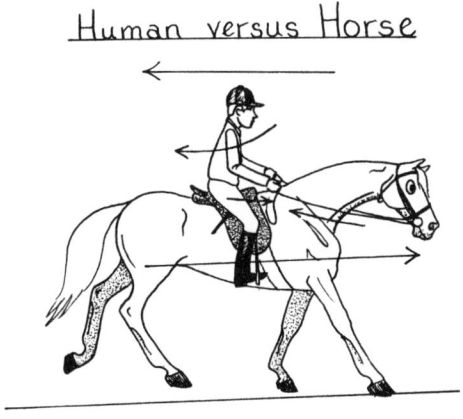

Human versus Horse

Canter

reins. This is evident with beginner riders where at every stride the snaffle bit is pulled one to two inches out of the side of the horse's mouth. Obviously, no horse can be on the bit like this. When this happens, we are really riding backward with our body and our arms, against the kinetics of the canter, exactly when the horse stretches the entire inside forward into the leading front leg. No wonder all the old cavalry regulations always talk of the allowing inside hand as the key to a good canter, but do little to explain more than "follow the motion of the horse."

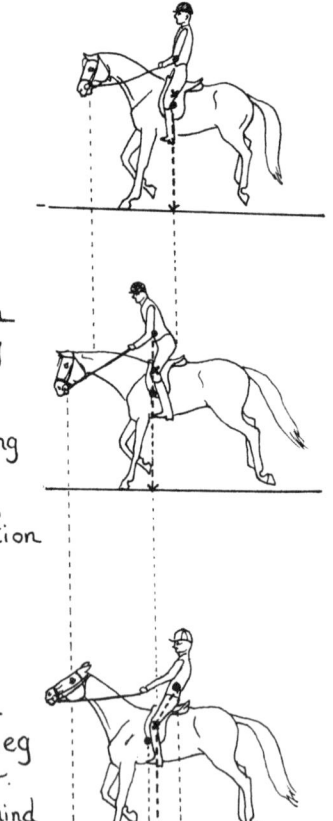

Working canter sitting
- center of gravity of horse and rider properly aligned
- effect of center of mass anticipated and contracted.

Working canter 2 point position
- horse's center of gravity slightly more forward properly aligned with center of gravity of rider.
- forward position of rider compensating for effect of center of mass
- human balance mechanism, ankle, knee, and hip joint absorbing motion of horse and keeping balance.

Working canter off balance
- the forward push by the hind leg not compensated by the rider.
- center of mass pulls rider behind center of gravity of the horse.
- horse going off the bit to maintain balance.

A practical way to teach a beginner to follow the movement of the horse with his inside shoulder and arms is to ask him to put the inside hand holding the rein solidly on his thigh, between the knee and hip. This forces the hip and shoulder to move together with the motion of the horse.

The forward movement of the thigh and hip is determined by the horse and is out of the rider's control. So with this technique, one is simply taking the arm, hand and shoulder along in the motion and conveying to the rider what he should be doing and what he should feel. It helps make the rider conscious that he is otherwise doing just the opposite, clutching the horse's mouth at the wrong moment of the movement. This clutch on the mouth makes it very difficult for the horse to balance himself back to the outside hind leg where the next canter stride starts with impulsion.

This technique works for the canter depart as well as for every subsequent canter stride. Remember, every canter stride is basically nothing else but a new canter depart.

If we now relate the position of the rider to his center of gravity, the effect of velocity and the center of mass to the center of gravity of the horse, we see that they all must be properly aligned. Accomplishing this must originate from the sensitivity of the seat and the impulses of balance to the rider's central nervous system which only gradually develops the proper reflexes to do so. This is all completely unique to riding; never do we encounter a similar requirement when standing on our feet.

ON THE THREE-BEAT CANTER

In competitive dressage, we recognize only the three-beat canter as correct. But if there is only one way to trot (and be called a trot), and three ways to walk (four-beat, pacing, and diagonal), then there are a large variety of canters, all of which are correct from the horse's point of view.

We have Western horses that lope, dressage horses who prefer a four-beat canter, a cross-canter, a lateral canter or a "false" canter. Then there is the completely different footfall of the full speed gallop of racehorses, not to even mention the *redopp* or *gallopade* of classical dressage. When you look at equestrian statues of emperors or famous generals in Europe, you may wonder what gait the horse is showing.

In competitive dressage we push the trot as far as the piaffe and passage, but not so far as to the *levade*. In the canter, though, we stop at the collected canter, with the definition that it must preserve the three-beat footfall. On the other hand, in classical dressage, we recognize the *gallopade*, a highly collected four-beat canter practically on the spot, and the *redopp*, a two-beat canter on the spot and the basis for airs above the ground. If you've watched a performance of the Spanish Riding School, you may have seen the horses bouncing back and forth on the spot prior to a *capriole* or a *ballotad*; that is the *redopp*.

However, the question can fairly be raised, "Is there truly a three-beat canter?" The answer depends on your visual perception, which in an average human is equivalent to about 22 frames per second. Anything faster than that is perceived not as an individual frame but instead as a fluid, continuous motion.

This human limitation of visual perception is the basis of seeing a movie as a continuous, fluid performance as more than 25-30 frames are played per second. Modern visual technology allows us to make up to 50 or 100 frames per second. And when we examine those films that show a horse in canter and analyze it frame by frame, we always find a four-beat canter. So, in reality, the definition of a four-beat canter depends on the visual acuity of the observer which explains why judges sometimes disagree among themselves. The rider, however, feels in his or her seat and knows what is going on under him or her.

Now since this three-beat canter is the only accepted canter in competitive dressage, we must make sure that our aids allow for these kinetics.

As we discussed earlier, the canter is a diagonal gait, either left hind to right front, or right hind to left front, depending on the lead. Our aids must integrate into this movement and must be different for the left or right leads.

As all horses are a bit crooked to either the left or right, the same as their humans who are not ambidextrous either, we often see fundamental problems of noncompatible kinetics of horse and rider. It is rare to see an absolutely straight canter at Third or Fourth Level, equally balanced left and right and with identical lateral movements or flying changes.

This becomes particularly visible when a series of flying changes is required, particularly when excessive restrictive aids in front lead to the haunches falling left or right, but to different degrees. It is here where Steinbrecht's "Ride your horse straight and forward" becomes crucially important as reflected in both the FEI and AHSA statements: "*In order not to restrict or restrain the lightness and fluency of the flying changes, the degree of collection should be slightly less than in a collected canter.*" This means more forward and less restraining hands, leading to a straight horse.

THE CANTER DEPART

There are dozens of recommendations on how to ride a canter or to ask for a canter depart, from the Pony Club approach of bending the horse to the outside, kicking with the outside leg and using to whip to make the poor thing go. On the other end of the scale is the approach that recognizes the kinetics of the situation.

From the kinetic point of view, it is clear that every canter stride is exactly the same as the first stride of the canter depart. Therefore, our aids, their sequence and their timing in relation to the kinetics are the same in the canter depart as they are to maintain the canter. The only part that may vary is the strength of the aids.

Since the first part of the canter is the push off from the engaged outside hind leg, it is also our outside leg that initiates the movement. But it should be kept as subtle as possible, more like a reminder, because otherwise the horse might interpret this outside leg aid as the key to cantering and that may give you a lot of trouble in the trot half passes when you use your outside leg and get a canter depart when you don't really want it.

Then, after the leg aid, following the diagonal impulsion the weight of the rider shifts from the centered position to putting the weight on the inside seatbone.

At this moment, the entire inside lowers and stretches forward, and the rider's seat, shoulders and hands must follow while the rider's inside leg encourages the stepping under of the horse's inside leg. Many experts advise that the inside aids are much more important than the outside leg to initiate and maintain the correct canter depart, when combined with the release of the inside reins. This is what is called an "allowing" hand in the literature.

When that is done correctly, the horse has the liberty to balance himself back over to the outside hind to start the same rhythm all over again.

CHAPTER 10

THE EFFECT OF WEIGHT, THE MOST SOPHISTICATED AID

In this chapter, we come back to our discussions in the beginning of this book, that is, the omnipresence of gravity and its effect on everything on this planet, including the horse and rider. But by understanding its effect, including now, hopefully, our riding, we no longer need be its victim but can make it a tool. We can use gravity for our purposes in a clear language that is perfectly understood by the horse if used correctly: these are the weight aids.

If you want to experience for yourself what the horse feels, get a backpack of more or less 20 pounds, and try to balance it well on your shoulders. Then have a friend shift the backpack to the left and you will see that, like it or not, you must compensate for the shift. You can compensate for the shift by

enlarging your stance or stepping sideways. Or, another way to keep the center of gravity in the middle of the base of support is to throw a compensatory weight such as a leg and arm out to the other side. This, however, is not feasible for the horse who cannot use his balancing pole to do so as he is held between the reins and on the bit.

Similarly, the horse will try to compensate for the rider's position on his back as the rider's weight influences the horse's balance from the moment the rider gets on the horse until he dismounts. The question is, are we just interfering with the horse, or are we suggesting to him his direction of movement by using our position deliberately to engage the combined center of gravity in one direction or the other or, putting it simply, by using our weight aids?

An outstanding European friend and rider admonished me many years ago, "Never push your horse around with crude aids—just take him with you and ride the movement you want ahead of him."

This notion has been recognized for centuries by outstanding riders and is much better expressed in the following short collection of quotes than I could possibly put it myself.

We begin with Robichon de la Guérinière, the founder of our present day dressage who accomplished the transition from the Ecole de Versailles to what we do today. It was he who clearly defined the shoulder-in, changed the saddle and based his riding on mental and physical harmony with the horse, as discussed in his book, **Ecole de Cavalerie,** 1729.

Above all he (the rider) will strive to prevent any unintentional changes of weight, as these are the gravest mistakes to be committed!

...The aids by weight are the most refined of all influences. Used unilaterally, they affect the position of the haunches, and bilaterally, they put the horse straight.

Here, a quote from Gustav Steinbrecht, whose book **The Gymnasium of the Horse (1876)** is still the foundation of German dressage training, as he refers to a shoulder-in:

In the shoulder-in the rider must therefore often work more with the outside rein and leg and even put his weight more on the outside so as to always remain in control and be able to determine the degree of sideways travel of the horse's outside legs, because the correct and unforced stepping over of the inside legs primarily depends on this.

Another clear recognition of the importance of the weight aids is also found in the **German Cavalry Regulations**. These regulations were first issued in 1882, at the time of Steinbrecht, Seeger and Plinzner, renewed in 1912, and the final edition was made in 1937, just before World War II. This last edition is popularly referred to as the **H.Dv 12**.

If the rider changes his weight to the right or the left, he creates an impulse to the horse to deviate into this direction, from the preceding line.

The mistaken inclination of most riders, is to act too much with their hands, and not enough with their legs or weight aids, and must be fought against continuously.

The ability to consistently coordinate the center of gravity of the rider with the continuously changing center of gravity of the horse and to maintain it there is the art to follow the movement of the horse.

If the rider changes his balance to the right or to the left, he induces the horse to deviate in this direction from the preceding line. This weight aid is executed by putting more weight on the corresponding seat bone. In doing so, the hip will slightly sink down and the knee position be a bit lower. A serious mistake is to collapse the hip as this causes a change of weight to the wrong side.

General Decarpentry, one of the most accomplished and educated riders of France and co-founder of the FEI, makes this reference to weight aids in his **Academic Equitation** (1949):

In lateral movements, the best manner in which the rider can conform to these conditions is by putting his weight on the stirrup that is on the side of the displacement. This causes his seat to shift slightly in the same direction and his body to lean imperceptibly that way also.

Similarly, Alois Podhajsky, Director of the Spanish Riding school in Vienna and a medal winner in the 1936 Olympics, has the following to say about weight aids in **The Complete Training of Horse and Rider** (1967):

When the weight of the body is transferred into the direction of the lateral movement, it will support the effect of the outside leg because the horse will try to step under the centre of gravity of the rider.

Then there is the practical application of this principal described by Nuno Oliveira for the shoulder-in, as written in his **Classical Principles of the Art of Training Horses** (1983):

Beware of the so-called shoulder-in, so frequently seen, in which the rider pulls on the inside rein while leaning on the same side, with his leg drawn back to jab the horse with the spur, which forces the poor animal to move laterally while twisted, and which takes all impulsion away from the horse, leading to resistance against the rider....
The weight should be on the outside buttock as the outside leg acts softly but firmly.

When you read Kyra Kyrlund's book **Dressage with Kyra** (1998), you'll find a wonderful summary of the same principles, too frequently forgotten in our present day dressage training of horse and rider.

The rider has the following means of communication or aids at his disposal: the LEG, the HAND (and the VOICE as a supplement to these), and last but not least, the WEIGHT (SEAT), which is the most important aid.

Whether the rider intends it or not, his WEIGHT influences the horse all the time. By weight I mean the central point or centre of gravity of the whole seat of the rider, which extends down from the chest through the stomach and pelvis into the thighs. Through muscle tone and body control of this middle part of the rider, the weight becomes the control centre of all influence. The response to all leg and hand signals is dependent on the position of the weight and the seat.

And, later, an excellent reminder,

However, it must not be forgotten that if it is easier to communicate with a sensitive horse, it is also easier for an alert and intelligent horse to learn bad habits.

It is probably not surprising that when the FEI rules were written by such figures as General Decarpentry, Dr. Gustav Rau, and General Halsing Berset in 1921, the basic concept of dressage was formulated not just as a sport, but the option of developing dressage into an art form. The recognition that weight is the most sophisticated and effective aid is clearly expressed in the following statement from the FEI.

The horse thus gives the impression of doing of his own accord what is required of him. Confident and attentive he submits generously to the control of his rider, remaining absolutely straight in any movement on a straight line and bending accordingly when moving on curved lines.

This statement does not refer to legs, hands, spurs, or whips, but to the invisible aids of weight, executed by putting more weight in one seat bone or the other, and by doing so, slightly shifting the center of gravity. This induces a well-trained horse to follow his natural response to correct the shift and, in so doing, execute exactly what the rider wants.

In the older literature, we see this expressed by the statement "putting more weight in one stirrup or the other." This should be done, however, without moving the seat and/or collapsing the hip, or by leaning in one direction or the other. The weight aids are not executed by shifting the seat, but by putting more weight on one seat bone or the other. The most common mistake of collapsing the hip does exactly the opposite of what we intend to do.

Now, when starting out a young horse, we must make a conscious decision to use weight as an aid from the very beginning, which requires a fairly sophisticated rider. It also requires that the rider feel where each leg is at any given moment. Too often riders rely on kicking, pulling and inflicting pain, teaching the horse in this process to completely disregard these types of aids and to simply avoid the pain as much as possible to execute the movements.

Looked at in this way, we see that the use of seat and weight are the only aids that are not based on the principle of inflicting pain. Instead, they use balance and natural reflexes in a much more sophisticated way to get what we want. However, not understanding either principle often leads to contradictory aids, confusing the horse and leading to resistance. This is particularly true when the weight of the rider tells the horse to go one way and the spurs, aids, and whip or reins force him to go in the other direction. Certainly we cannot expect a free, forward moving, light and elegant movement executed under such circumstances. Ballerinas are not trained by the ballet master wielding a whip and a poke.

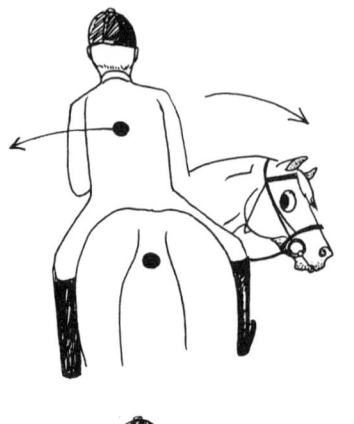

The horse will compensate with his head and neck for the one-sided position of the rider.

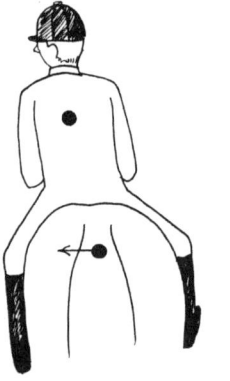

The horse who is on aids will follow the change of center of gravity.

Returning to practical considerations, let's look at what happens when we put a rider on a horse who is standing still and square, assuming we use an educated, sophisticated rider who knows where his seat and weight is in relation to the horse.

1. The horse does not change his natural center of gravity; it remains where it used to be prior to the rider mounting.

2. The rider's center of gravity and mass is definitely well above the horse depending on how tall and heavy the upper body of the rider is.

The Effect of Weight, The Most Sophisticated Aid

Side view

3. Also, the saddle is above the horse's center.

Conclusion: This creates a new center of gravity of the combined masses which is higher than the original one of the horse.

As a result:
1. The balance becomes more delicate since the center of gravity and the center of mass are higher above the base of support than before.

2. Therefore, the subcortical reflexes for balance must be readjusted and become more fine tuned for the new situation.

Looking at the situation vertically, we can draw the following conclusion:

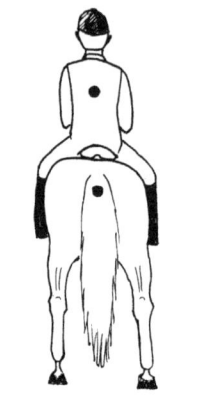

Wide stance in balance

1. The rider's leaning forward or backward will never really throw the horse off balance, but clearly can effect the horse in the way he moves.

2. But lateral changes by the rider (leaning out to one side or the other) become more intrusive or disturbing to the horse. And the narrower the horse's stance, the more any lateral change of the center of gravity demands an immediate response from the subcortical reflex mechanism of the horse to maintain the center over its base of support.

So we see that the higher the new center of gravity, the more delicate its balance is, depending directly on the narrowness of the horse's stance. A wide horse is less affected whereas a narrow horse is immediately affected by anything related to the position of the rider, which, if used correctly, can become extremely effective as an aid.

We see this consistently in the halt at X where very often the horse steps out behind because of the position and unequal seat of the rider. The horse is just trying to rearrange the center of gravity under the rider's seat bones. So remember, irrespective of how we sit on the horse, we influence the center of gravity. This can be helpful or disruptive to the balance of the horse,

The Effect of Weight, The Most Sophisticated Aid

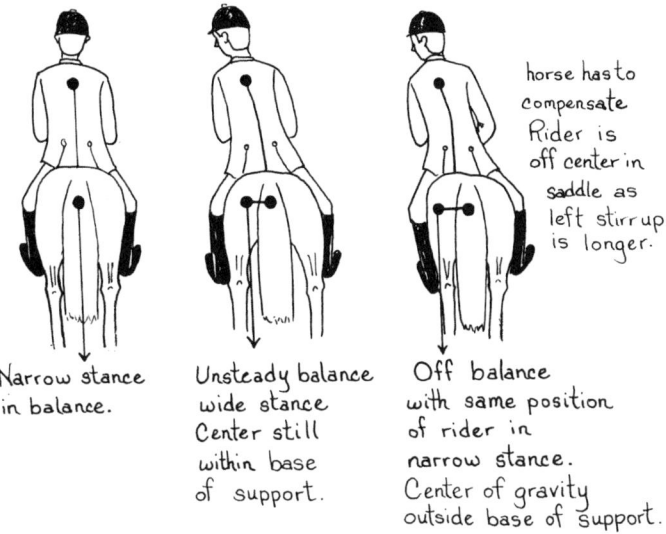

Narrow stance in balance.

Unsteady balance wide stance Center still within base of support.

Off balance with same position of rider in narrow stance. Center of gravity outside base of support.

horse has to compensate. Rider is off center in saddle as left stirrup is longer.

depending on what we are doing. Above all, we must be very conscious of what we do to the horse and that the reaction of the horse is to keep the center of gravity within the support base.

You must master the total coordination of your legs and hands from a confirmed seat in all three gaits before you can begin to master the techniques for using the weight aids. The techniques are actually very simple, extremely effective and more easily executed than the other aids. The tricky part is that they are based on a seat in complete harmony with the horse's kinetics and a full understanding on the part of the rider of what is going on under him.

If you consider the horse and rider as a unit, the head of the rider is the highest point. The human head weighs approximately 25 pounds and so just looking to the right or to the left shifts 25 pounds in this direction. As a normal reaction in turning the head, we also lower the shoulder on the same side a bit,

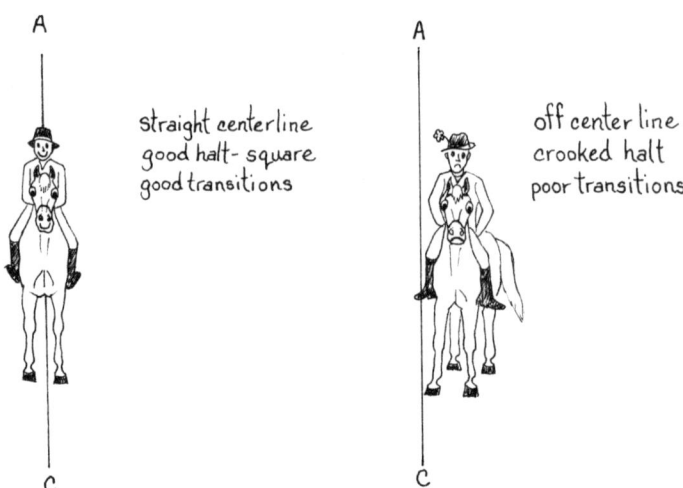

Weight of rider to left and left stirrup longer — most frequently seen in competition.

Result   horse drifting left
         not square
         haunches falling in, compensating for one-sided position of rider.

Correction - shorten stirrup left side
            watch your position
            whip or spurs will not help as they don't correct alignment of center of gravity.

which puts additional weight on the seat bone, lowers the hip of the corresponding side and puts more weight on the corresponding seat bone.

But, if you watch riders in dressage, as a group they seem to have a fixation on the ears of the horse, and never look at the position and point of where they should be going or really want to go.

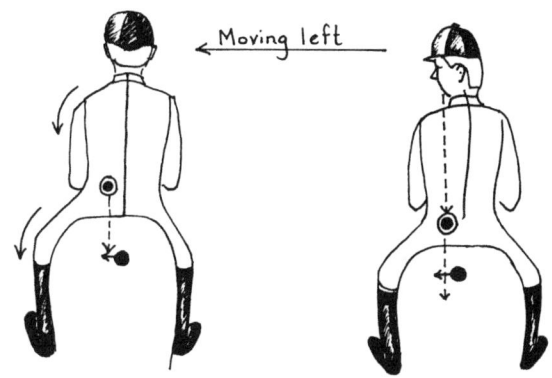

Weight in stirrup on left
- lower left shoulder
- raise right pelvis
- looking still straight
- horse will leg yield or half pass

Positioning head and looking in direction of movement shifts approximately 25 pounds to left without changing basic position.

Both can be combined if needed. Usually done by hunter and jumper riders. The horse follows your eyes and where you look.

On the other hand, hunter/jumper and Western riders always look where they want to go or where the next jump is, changing unconsciously their weight distribution, which is then simply followed by the horse. That is the basis of the saying for teaching young riders to jump, "just look where you want to go and the horse follows your eyes."

Understanding these principles and the effect of gravity on kinetics can make dressage riding almost effortless, a mutually shared pleasure between horse and rider and the decisive step in the direction to develop a true expression of art.

Weight shifts to the outside and distorts the position of the rider becoming asymetric and weight aid opposes intention of rider leading to spur, whip, and hand riding.
= Contradictory aids.

OUR CONCLUSION

To summarize the specific concepts outlined in this book, we realize that we are working on and hopefully improving the natural kinetics of the horse. Conversely, in making a good rider we must eliminate our own natural human kinetics and replace them with new horse-oriented ones. This "reprogramming" is relatively easy in the early part of life, but becomes more difficult and limited in possible outcome when growing up.

No wonder it takes six years to make a Grand Prix horse, but a lifetime to learn to ride!

EPILOGUE

I hope that the considerations touched on in this book will help riders and instructors take a look at the problems they are facing and approach them with new ways of thinking. I also hope the book itself will not be a huge flop for my nice editor!

Insight usually develops with age and being at the stage where, as the saying goes, it takes two lifetimes to learn to ride becomes a reality, I am fully aware of all the shortcomings of these pages, and only hope that others will pick up the concept and will elaborate or think thoughts for the benefit of all riders. For the rest, I will continue enjoying my horses who have patiently taught me so much, especially Prinz, who accomplished my membership in the Century Club where we reached a combined total of 115 years being still relatively sound of body and mind.

Central New York Dressage and Combined Training Association

Annual Meeting and Luncheon
Saturday, November 18th
Cazenovia College Equine Education Center

11am-Noon   Annual Meeting

- ★ Greeting and welcome!
- ★ Financial report

New initiatives/committee reports
★ Voting for 2001 Board of Directors
★ Introductions of new board members
★ Volunteers for 2001 programs and shows
★ Awards Dinner in late winter/early spring 2001
★ Member feedback and discussion

Noon-1pm   Lunch

1pm-2:30pm   Lecture by Dr. Max Gahwyler

*CNYD&CTA Logo clothing and other items available for sale today;
Signed copies of Dr. Gahwyler's most recent publication also for sale.*